HAPPY

The author, one year old.

Happy With My Lot

Edith Scott

Pentland Books
Edinburgh · Cambridge · Durham

First published in 2001 by
Pentland Books
1 Hutton Close
South Church
Bishop Auckland
Durham

British Library Cataloguing in Publication Data.
A catalogue record for this book is available
from the British Library.

ISBN 1 85821 934 5

Typeset by George Wishart & Associates, Whitley Bay.
Printed and bound by Antony Rowe Ltd., Chippenham.

Acknowledgements

I would like to thank Christine, a good friend who encouraged me to go ahead with this book.

Preface

Does it really matter
If your rival gets ahead
Or someone scores a point from you
By something done or said?

Does it really matter
If you're left a bit behind
Don't give other people
A chance to wreck your peace of mind?

Does it really matter
If you never reach the top
Don't turn life into a rat race
And run until you drop?

Be content, don't ask too much
Nor aim too high
For the things that really matter
Are the things you cannot buy.

One may wonder how I could say that I am happy with my lot, as every movement hurts somewhere, every action an effort, and I never go out, but some of us are blessed with a contented nature that enables us to cope and accept our disabilities.

July 1985

The Beginning

For a long time now I have thought of writing my life story. It has not been a very eventful life but everyone's life is different. I don't suppose it will be read by many people but for young readers some incidents might prove interesting about the way we used to live.

I was born in 1912 on January 27th in the early hours of a cold and snowy morning. My parents had engaged a nurse for a month.

My mother was not over fond of children so I was not planned for, but I happened, as a matter of fact my parents were saving up for a half-hoop diamond ring.

We lived at 93, Englefield Road, Islington, North London, quite a nice neighbourhood at that time, in a top flat in a large house; they had to go down to the first floor for every drop of water and to the hall floor for the toilet. My bassinette used to stand in the large hall.

They were nice people in the house, the householders were a middle aged couple and their daughter, the mother was in an invalid chair.

On the first floor were a couple who had had two children and lost them at birth, they were a Mr and Mrs Rowley. She went out to business and at weekends I was as much in their flat as in our own, they made a fuss of me and I was very unhappy when occasionally they went away to her sisters at Southall. While we lived there my father and the other two gentlemen were called to serve on a jury.

Now I must go back in time to my parents' background, my mother's father was a compositor on a newspaper. I cannot

Grandma. Mrs Cawley aged 63.

recall what it was called (*The Westminster Gazette* I think). He had served seven years apprenticeship and did work for the War Office and Foreign Office and earned a good salary. He devoted all his spare time to Packington Street Methodist Church, he was choir master and secretary for forty-five years till he died.

My grandma was a milliner, they met at Sunday School at the same church when they were three, they married when they were both twenty-three, my grandma wore a dress of mauve and cream silk, in later years I made myself a blouse of the cream silk.

My mother was born a year later and was their only child, she had lovely wavy auburn hair and a temper to go with it. I have a tiny photo which I cherish where her parents look so placid and she looks a bit of a terror in a little round straw hat. She attended a church school, previously a school where they taught pot hooks and hangers.

2

My mother's father, Mr Cawley.

One day when her mother was having the sweep, she came out of school because she wanted to see him but he had already gone and she was disappointed. As she got older she did a lot of work collecting money for missionaries, and I still have a bible that was given to her.

She was in the choir and had a very nice voice and was also a Sunday-school teacher. My mother's parents moved from Islington to Clissold Road, Stoke Newington by the park; they wanted a larger house because my mother's grandpa and Aunt Sarah made their home with them. Old grandpa had been a chemist and his sister Aunt Sarah a ladies' maid, she was very precise. So now there were five in the house and they had a woman to help with the work. Her name was Esther and she worked for us for years and was a good and faithful person.

My mother never went out to business, she said if she had she would have liked to have been a secretary. She had a very easy life and would go out with her mother or friends most afternoons and buy material for blouses etc. which she made up. She hardly ever went to Packington Street dressed in the same thing twice. They had visits from Ministers to talk over church matters with her father.

Destiny

It was while they were living in Clissold Road that my mother met my father. It happened like this, on the opposite side of the road there lived a young lady who waited at the bus stop, my mother thought she looked such a nice person that one day she put a note in her letter-box to ask her if she would like to come over for a cup of tea, she was pleased to accept and they became friends. Her name was Kate, she had a young man, Walter, who was a barman in a city wine house. Her idea was to introduce my mother to another young man who worked there called William, they were introduced and it was a case of love at first sight. At the time mother was dressed in mourning for an aunt.

19 Maury Road, Stoke Newington (corner house) where mum was married from.

Church where my parents were married (now flats) Maury Road.

In those days one wore mourning for about a year for a close relative, then into half-mourning, black edged handkerchiefs, jet jewellery and you used black edged envelopes.

In the course of time mother went to William's home where she met his father, who was a porter at Merchant Taylor's College, his brother and three sisters; my father was the eldest, his mother having died at the age of forty-two, when he was seventeen. They were a very different family from my mother's and were on the poor side.

Now, in my mother's home they were very much against alcohol, only keeping a little brandy in the house for medicinal purposes. I often wonder how they felt about my mother meeting a young man in such a place. However, when they met him they liked him very much as did most people, he was quiet, shy and gentle. They had hoped she might marry someone from the church but such is fate.

My father's working hours were very long, early morning till late at night, no Sundays. It was a wine house where they sold spirits but not like a normal public house where they sold beer. The only way my mother could see him was to meet him on his early turn at Dalston Junction, she left the house sometimes when her father had gone to bed, returning late, my father having seen her home and taking a tram ride back to Dalston where he lived. They always sent a picture postcard to each other every day, in those days you could buy sets of six postcards, I still have some lovely ones. I guess the postman must have looked out for them. I have recently destroyed a box of love letters.

My mother liked my father's father and the eldest sister, Alie, best out of the family. Another sister was what you might call the black sheep of the family, she could not be trusted with money, my father would leave her money to pay his insurance and she would spend it. Her idea of sweeping a room was to sweep the dirt under the rug, she became an unmarried mother.

*(Auntie Alie) Alice and her mother-in-law
Mrs Ruile (dad's sister).*

My father was very good to his family and would give them money if they were short, they even pestered him for money after he was married and I was born. My mother was very fond of her sister-in-law, Alie, and I can remember going to see her after her baby, Alice was born, I was four then. On another occasion we went to tea and we had some fairy cakes and I was somewhat fascinated by the cake papers which I took home. By the way, I still have a walking stick of Grandpa Scott's which was presented to him when he retired.

About this time my mother's parents moved to Maury Road, Stoke Newington on the borders of Clapton, a corner house with a large garden, the stairs and rooms were already covered with Wilton carpet. My mother was married from this house, the church being only a few yards away but they had a carriage and two grey horses, my father wore a high hat my mother a costume, the year was 1909, she was twenty-eight and my father twenty-six, and they had been courting for three years. They were married on Christmas Day.

In 1912 I was born and was to be an only child like my mother. I would have liked an older brother but really have had no regrets, what you don't have you don't miss.

My mother had a very easy confinement. I was christened when I was six weeks old at Packington Street church, Edith Florence Emily, Florence after my mother and Emily after Grandma.

The First War

When I was about three years old my mother found out I had been born on the Kaiser's birthday and she wasn't at all pleased. I was a good child by all accounts, one thing I liked to do was turn on the gas taps on the gas stove, they were brass in those days and easy to turn. One day I was in the garden and pulled the head off a flower and was reprimanded by the daughter of the house. When at I was two and a half, in 1914, the Great War

Schraders Wine Merchants where dad worked
in Colman Street and Mason's Avenue.

started on August 4th. My father was eventually called up but not accepted owing to a very severe ulcerated leg, a wound the size of the palm of the hand which he had got as a boy. One day when the road was being repaired he climbed over some stones and fell and hurt his leg, his mother did not clean it properly and it healed up with some grit in it and turned into an ulcer. The doctor recommended a year's rest but as they were short of money they sent him out to work, first to a gentleman's outfitters, which he would have liked to remain in, then apprenticed him to the wine trade (Licensed Victuallers) which paid better in the city. It was the worst type of occupation, he was always on his feet and had that bad leg till the time he died and was nearly always in pain. Neglect like that would not be allowed in these days.

He spent a small fortune on various ointments and went to several hospitals; one recommended amputation. He also went to the German hospital where they refused to treat him because he was English.

During my early years I used to sit at the kitchen window and watch the soldiers go by, marching along singing 'It's a long way to Tipperary'. At other times there were flocks of sheep going to be slaughtered. The first word I attempted to say was bi-be-cul for bicycle, my mother said what a hard word to start on.

If there was an air raid coming they would call out, 'Take Cover' and when it was over 'All Clear'.

If it happened in the night I would be wrapped in a blanket and we went downstairs in the cellar my father generally had some sugared almonds or sweets of some kind. Of an evening mother would take me to dad's place in the city and we would sit in a little office. If we had a raid while there dad would lock up the premises, he was now manager, and we would go and shelter in a bank vault. Coming home we took the 76 bus, the buses in those days had open tops and if it rained they had tarpaulin over the seats.

The author aged eighteen months.

Air-raids though bad were nothing to be compared with the last war but we did have bombed houses; one house in Ball's Pond Road, Dalston, was hit when an old couple were kneeling in prayer. We saw the German airship brought down in flames from our kitchen window at Cuffley, Potters Bar, August 1916, it was a Zeppelin.

One day while out shopping with my mother I went into the tea-grocers and helped myself to some biscuits while she was in another shop. They used to have seven pound biscuit tins all

The author aged five years.

along the front of the counter nice and handy, but they didn't mind as my mother was a customer and they all had a good laugh.

We had three milk deliveries a day, in the early morning a can of milk, oval in shape with a handle, then during the morning the milkman would call and you took it in a jug, the milkman ladled it out of a churn, then again in the afternoon. We had service in those days, postal deliveries several times a day and the postman always knocked.

The street cries of London have long since died out, women singing out 'Sweet Lavender', the Muffin Man with a tray on his head covered with a cloth, chair menders and knife grinders and plenty of beggars singing for a few coppers, cats' meat man, rag and bone carts, organ grinders, sandwich board men, and water carts that sprayed the gutters, and pavement artists with their lovely crayon pictures which all vanished as soon as it rained.

There were plenty of horses about with their nosebags, being led to a horse trough to have a drink, what I didn't like to see was them slipping on the icy roads. If anyone was seriously ill they would put straw down in the road to deaden the sound of horses' hooves.

It was nice going shopping in the High Street on a Saturday evening when the shops were open very late and the stalls had naphtha lamps (naked lights). During the war years, if I remember rightly, one evening, we heard the Silvertown explosion. My mother gave one of her screams which she was prone to do when frightened and always said she felt better after that. I might say anyone around her did not, she once gave a scream over something when she was living at home and Aunt Sarah said she felt ill for three days. Poor Aunt Sarah, one night my mother slept with her and she had a dream that she was driving a pony and trap and kept saying 'Gee up! Gee up!' and hit her aunt on the nose.

I had some very nice presents given to me as a child from some of dad's customers, he was well liked and I suppose that was their way of showing their appreciation; one was a pretty tea service, some nicely bound books and a needlework basket in pale blue wickerwork shaped like a motor car. I first went to a private school where one Saturday morning we had an air-raid and all the windows were broken. During the war years we went to Worthing for our summer holidays, they didn't have raids there. When the war was over we moved to Chesholm Road, Stoke Newington and here our life style changed drastically.

The Miracle

At last the war was over but at the end of 1918 and beginning of 1919 we had a very severe influenza epidemic which it is said killed more people than in the Great War; people were dying all around, doctors were overworked and used to visit late at night. My mother went in to see a neighbour next door who had it and while there the lady died. A few days later my mother was taken ill and had complications, influenza, bronchitis, pneumonia and pleurisy; she was delirious and the doctor only gave her three days to live. Grandma came to look after her, going home late at night when dad came home and returning early next morning when dad went off to work. She was a very good woman and did all she could. My parents were not quite teetotal and therefore kept a little whisky in the house, my mother in her delirium asked Grandma for the whisky, she poured half a glass and drank it and slept for seven hours. My grandma was terribly worried and thought she would never wake again. When dad came home he said she should not have let her have it, but their prayers were answered and she woke up feeling much better and had lost her cough, the doctor was puzzled and thought she had made a miraculous recovery, I don't know if they ever told him. As she was getting better I can remember hearing outside the bedroom door the doctor asking her to say ninety-nine, repeat ninety-nine. So in some cases alcohol can work wonders, but I can quite understand people being against it for the misery and distress it has caused in many homes where men spent on drink their wages which were badly needed for the home.

When people abuse a thing that's when trouble starts, be it food, drink or anything else. I was seven at the time and remember washing the kitchen floor. My mother was ill for six weeks. When fully recovered and able to go out her father gave her a fur collar and muff which he had bought from a furrier who was a member of our church. The people downstairs were very good at this time and my parents gave the lady a leather handbag.

During our time in Chesholm Road, about 1922, some people who lived opposite us had a dairy business and were related to either Edith Thompson or Frederich Bywater who were involved in a murder case.

For my eighth birthday my parents gave me a nice doll's pram, I had had three prams, as a baby my mother exchanged one for another type as time went on. Also my grandparents gave me a piano, I think it cost £40, they thought I was a nice age to start learning to play but alas I was not interested and never practised. I have often thought what a golden opportunity that would have been for someone with talent.

I had all the children's usual ailments, measles, chicken-pox, whooping-cough and scarlet fever but was not very ill with any of them.

School Days

I went to Church Street School in Stoke Newington and for the most part liked it. I was a slow learner but what patience the teachers had. I can recall them all: Miss Hunter, Miss Gotley, Miss Butler, Miss Dee and Mrs Thatcher were my favourites, Mrs Suffling the head mistress who was quite the lady always wore a becoming long dress and had auburn hair. I love auburn hair and even now am attracted to it whenever I see a child with it.

Anyway I managed to come fourth in a class of between fifty and sixty, classes were very large in those days, too large. The thing I was most interested in was needlework, especially embroidery. While at school I had embroidered two nun's veiling night-dresses for the headmistress. I had some nice prizes from school, six books and a needlework basket given for Good Conduct, Trustworthiness, Needlework, Drawing and Painting and Composition.

While in the infants we were asked to write out the Lord's

In the Infants. Jack Nursey and the author.

Prayer. Have you ever tried to write what a classroom of children mumble out? I didn't known one word from the other, my teacher must have had a good laugh.

It used to be the rule if you found anything in the playground or elsewhere you would take it round to all the classes to find the owner. On one or two occasions I fancied a walk round and took my own handkerchief and someone always claimed it. There was a boy, Jack Nursey, who lived in the same road as me and was in my class; he used to chase me coming home from school so, to give myself a head start, I would collect my hat and coat from the cloakroom not stopping to put them on till I got on my own doorstep then ring the bell for my mother to let me in.

I was never allowed out in the street to play but could have friends in or go to their house. I also had some nice birthday parties. Mr and Mrs Clifford came up from downstairs and he was a tease and kept tormenting me, in the end I hit him on the cheek with my blancmange spoon.

In our last year of schooling we went to laundry and cookery classes, I upset the laundry mistress once by rinsing a woollen vest in cold water.

At cookery once we had to prepare fish and had to cut the head off, I didn't fancy doing it and asked the girl next to me if she would cut it off but she wouldn't, I forget what happened.

I always liked Empire Day and one year was asked to be Britannia because I suppose I had long dark hair.

I was now approaching fourteen and about to leave school, there was talk about entering for a Trade Scholarship but as my arithmetic was not good that fell through.

I did so want an autograph book so my mother bought one for me so that my teachers might enter a verse in it. I cried the day I left school.

Just before I left I had a new hat and coat, bottle green and looked quite grown up as I had grown quickly at that age, anyway a little girl made me a curtsy.

My mother said she had made up her mind that I was to have six months freedom between school and work which I enjoyed very much and several times a week would go to Sharp's Needlework Shop for silks and transfers. A skein of silk at that time cost $1^1/_2$d in old money, now at time of writing, they are about 35p (seven shillings in old money) I have a large box full at the present time which is worth about £200. (Now 51p, 1996)

Sometimes we would go to the cinema in the afternoons and they would bring round tea on a tray.

Some Saturday afternoons we would go to the pictures with grandpa who nearly always fell asleep. As a family we were always fond of the cinema except Grandma who didn't care for it. When I was young we would go home to grandma's for tea and she had made me a figure of a man in pastry, these were happy days.

Dark Days

Now to go back a few years. When I was nine everything went wrong with our little world, my father lost his job, he had been in the city and with the same company in Colman Street and Gresham Street for twenty-one years and was manager when they suddenly changed hands and the new owners brought all their own staff. We never thought this state of affairs would last six years, it was the beginning of those awful years of depression. In 1921 there were 2,508,000 unemployed and work was hard to get, preference being given to ex-servicemen which was only right, but my father was not a fit man. It was not for the want of trying but he could not find regular work anywhere.

There was no such thing as redundancy money in those days. Unemployment money was inadequate, I think it was seventeen shillings for the man, five shillings for his wife and one shilling for each child. Our rent was fifteen shillings a week so after that was paid we were left with the sum total of eight shillings for everything.

After a certain time the allowance was reduced and you were issued with vouchers for coal, milk and groceries. This state of affairs to my mother, who had never wanted for anything, was a nightmare – and to my father – well there is nothing more degrading to a breadwinner than not to be able to supply the fundamental needs of his family.

After my parents' savings had gone mother's parents helped in many ways. One year grandpa and grandma had a fortnight at Clacton and paid for us to have a week with them. I remember going by a very early train and arriving there in time for breakfast.

They say troubles never come singly, indeed there was another shock to come; my grandpa had a fall in the church the schoolroom really, he hurt his leg and was laid up for some time; then he got appendicitis, it got to the stage when it was a matter of twenty-four hours, he had the operation in Mildmay Hospital and it had to be paid for in those days.

While in hospital a male nurse did not treat him nicely and this worried him. After coming home, during convalescence he became morbid and got neurasthenia (a nervous disease). Once a man who had led such an active and busy life he didn't know how to occupy his time and one day grandma just caught him in time as he was about to swallow some carbolic, he was then sent to a mental hospital at Southgate. Although only nine I remember going to see him in three hospitals, he later died at Southgate aged sixty-three on November 9th. I can remember the funeral, it being dusk on our return and the carriages having lamps on the side. Grandma bought some ground at Finchley Cemetery for six, that was for grandpa, grandma, mum, dad, me and my husband if I married. As it turned out only grandpa, grandma and dad are buried there, my mother being cremated. It is a lovely cemetery, so vast that on Sundays they have a bus to take you to different parts.

My grandpa had had some lovely presentations made to him during his life at the church from time to time, an illuminated address, a silver and green sugar bowl, silver teapot, silver fruit stand with green glass bowl which I still cherish and a music cabinet which we gave to cousin Walter who was organist at his church.

During his illness my grandpa had received a printer's pension but grandma hadn't realized that on his death this would terminate. Grandpa hadn't been one to save, so we were now all in the same boat, one couldn't help the other, grandma only had the widow's pension of ten shillings and the residue of her savings. This same year my father's father died of bronchitis.

As time went on grandma put in for a printer's pension, this was acquired by votes and we went to the Connaugh Rooms to receive them. Our own position was deteriorating, we now owed some rent and were served with a notice to quit on my mother's forty-third birthday. My mother had two male cousins, Ernest and Walter, both in very good positions; one was an estate agent and his wife a school teacher with no family, the other an accountant and his wife the Principal of a girls' school, they had two children. As I was about to have an endowment out in about six months time my mother wrote to cousin Ernest, who hadn't any family, to ask if he could advance the equivalent amount of the endowment and when we received the same we would repay him. He replied and said he couldn't see his way clear to lending us the money as he had a lot of expenses. They were churchgoers and I suppose they considered themselves Christians, perhaps he forgot years ago his mother borrowed money from Aunt Sarah to buy their house. It didn't cause a rift to our friendship, years later he sent us a calendar with a verse by Charles Kingsley about helping lame dogs over stiles, what a short memory he had! In the end our church helped us, there is a lot of truth in the saying when one door closes another opens. Many years after I used to send things for the church bazaar, one year a whole suitcase of hand-embroidered articles, I felt that in some way I had helped to repay them for their kindness.

About this time we were invited to a cousin's wedding, a friend of mother's had given her a cream dress and she dyed it a pale blue, my grandma who had been a milliner had some grey lace and made her a hat with a blue rose in it. My mother looked as nice as anyone, all for the total sum of a fourpenny Drummer dye.

Another good friend we had was the lady I used to spend so much time with in Englefield Road, she took us out one day and bought me a dress and coat.

Her sister who had two girls and lived in Southall offered for me to spend a week there. I went but my mother, who could not bear to part with me, cried nearly all week, my father said he never wanted to go through another week like that.

My birthday card 1945.

After my mother married and great grandpa and Aunt Sarah had died my grandparents moved to 112, Brooke Road, not far from Maury Road, another corner house. Eventually we went to live there too but alas it didn't last long as my mother had never got on with her own mother.

I can remember everything in that home, the kitchen with its gas stove beautifully polished standing on a hearth stone slab with its steel band rubbed clean with emery paper, the bars of household soap cut up ready for use so it could harden, and the view out of the window to the large garden with a row of poplar trees in the distance. The sitting room with its prickly covered horse-hair suite that was mahogany, the piano, the what-not in the corner with its various ornaments, one a Chinese mandarin with a nodding head, the religious pictures on the wall, one, 'The Light of the World' the other Jesus walking on the water, and books each side of the fireplace, there were about six shelves of books each side, all the poets, Dickens, encyclo-paedias and countless others. The brass kerb and fire irons. Oh, what a lot of work! It was a corner house with a pillar-box on the opposite side and a gas lamp on our corner which the lamp lighter would come along and light. There used to be an old lady in a bonnet and large apron sitting on a wooden box who used to sweep the crossing for a few coppers.

During the six years my father was out of work he did get short term employment from time to time, Christmas time he worked delivering letters and got good money, another time he was a canvasser for the Sterilized milk company in Culford Road. He once had a very unusual job, it was called Quin-quennial, to do with five-yearly valuation; he had to be in a public house and be in a position where he could watch the till and memorize the takings, all expenses paid of course.

During his spare time, as he was very fond of painting, he painted Christmas and birthday cards and sold some for 3d each (old money). A great friend of ours who lived in Huddersfield used to have about three dozen at Christmas. My mother also had a sample book of Christmas cards which we took round to friends for them to order, private cards with your name and address printed; one friend who was a lampshade maker and had her own workshop in Petherton Road gave me a lot of silk pieces. I was delighted and also received a lot of pocket money.

After a time we sold the piano which after all was never used and also a gold bracelet of my mother's. A few years before she died I bought her another one.

Living in Brooke Road meant crossing a very busy High Street to go to school, it was a twenty minutes walk each way, four times a day for my mother and sometimes dad – how they looked after me.

One evening we went to see my dad's uncle and aunt who lived in Richmond Road and they gave me some money to go and buy some sweets. On the way home a man spoke to me and said some horrible things to me and would I like to go for a

Dad's card, for my birthday 1942.

walk. I knew something was wrong and quickly said 'Go away! Go away!' and he did. Just a few yards away led to London Fields, to think I was always taken care of then just for once on my own I nearly ran into danger.

We heard about this time the tragic news of Kate, the young woman who had brought my parents together. She had killed herself by throwing herself out of the window, leaving her husband and two little girls.

Some friends of my grandparents who lived in the next road,

Christmas 1950, for mum and me.

had three daughters and the family were members of Northwold Methodist church. I used to go along with them some Sunday mornings to the service, one morning I fainted. I have always been subject to fainting for various reasons, sometimes for no apparent reason, once at a first-aid lesson at school, at the greengrocers, the chiropodists and again in Church not many years ago. The first time was when my mother had a poisoned finger and she went to the doctor's and he lanced it, as a matter of act it didn't hurt her but I thought it did and promptly fell on the floor. The doctor said leave her there, she will be alright.

I hate to think of anyone being hurt either physically or mentally.

In those days young people were kept in total ignorance

about the facts of life. The word 'sex' was never spoken about and if you enquired where babies came from you were probably told such nonsense as under the gooseberry bush. I had noticed from the window a lady who used to pass by, she seemed to get stouter and stouter until one day she had got remarkably thinner and was pushing a pram. I put two and two together and that's how I found out.

My mother, whose hair was so long she could sit on it, thought the weight of it might be the reason for causing her so many headaches so decided to have it cut off. She had it shingled at Chalks the hairdressers near Abney Park. My dad was most upset and so was her mother, all that beautiful long wavy auburn hair, cut off. I have a lock of it and treasure it. It didn't help her headaches at all, nearly every morning she would wake up with a sick head and couldn't do much till it had passed off, now they call it migraine. I too used to have a lot of headaches when young, now I am thankful to say I never get one. Once when young I had a permanent headache for nearly two months and didn't know what to do with myself, I couldn't take an interest in anything and can remember mum saying, don't do anything silly will you?

In my spare time I used to make hats for friends, at that time you could get a buckram shape and a bundle of straw about an inch wide and cover it, add some flowers and you had a pretty hat.

We moved from Brooke Road to Northwold Road number 93, twice I have lived at a number 93 and 112. We only stayed there for about two years, at that time it was very difficult to find accommodation. While there I went to work at a machine embroidery firm at 2¼p per hour (ten and tenpence per week) and 10d deducted for a morning and afternoon cup and tea. I didn't stay there long because it being machine embroidery meant I was not interested. During this time we had a very cold spell, one morning it looked as if it had been raining but it was black ice and scores of people fell and broke their limbs, it was known as 'Icy Wednesday'. I walked to Stamford Hill with a struggle and slipped down outside the firm and fainted.

A Silver Lining

We moved from Northwold Road to Narford Road, Clapton, number 30, this was about 1926, the year of the General Strike. Whenever there was an election my father would work for the Conservative Party, their headquarters were at No 25, Dalston Lane. On one occasion Sir Robert Gower was the candidate and he won. Two unusual names concerning this election: the agent's name was Eatwell and his son-in-law was Mr Beer. My father went canvassing and mother and I addressed envelopes. Some time later my father worked with a man named Drinkwater.

While working on the election my father was introduced to a Mrs Smith who was to be our benefactor. Her husband was a director of the Star Laundry at Hackney Downs, she spoke to her husband and my father was offered a job as a time keeper in the garage and one night a week to fill in when the night-watchman had his night off. He also painted the numbers and letters on the laundry hampers and took their dog for a walk every morning and did their gardening, so at last our troubles were over.

They were good to us and gave us our first wireless set and paid the licence. Although very kind she was of a Jekyll and Hyde nature and could be very arrogant.

I mentioned earlier that my mother had lovely auburn hair and a temper to go with it. It's a blessing my father and I had placid natures or I don't know what would have happened. As a child I was rather frightened of her when she was in a rage but later got to understand.

I once had a rust crêpe-de-chine dress with rows of narrow velvet ribbon round hem and sleeves, it was the sweetest dress and I suppose I kept on saying how nice it was and it got on her nerves for she tore it in threads. I was heartbroken and when she realized what she had done she was so sorry, after many tears shed all was forgiven but never forgotten.

By nature she was very lovable, sensitive and easily hurt, could not hide her feelings and was never secretive. If anyone annoyed her a look with those blue eyes, well! you have heard the saying, 'If looks could kill'. Despite all the trauma we went through although you can almost hate a person, you can still love them.

While living at Narford Road, wonder of wonders, we had electricity installed! How lovely, no more delicate gas mantles to put on and no more irons to heat on the gas stove.

In 1930 we moved to 152 Amhurst Road, the Star Laundry had bought two houses and had them converted into four self contained flats in each house for some of their workers. As my father had twenty minutes walk across the Downs they offered us one of them. I said, 'Are we going to live in Hackney?' We preferred Clapton. Anyway we moved there in 1930 and stayed till 1966.

In 1934 my parents celebrated their silver wedding and I gave mother a silver watch and dad a silver cigarette case with his initials engraved on it.

In 1935 my grandma died in Hackney Hospital from dropsy. Mum and I were there, the 26th January, the day before my 23rd birthday, it was a snowy Saturday evening and she was born in a snow storm. She had been a very good woman despite bad health, when young she had rheumatic fever and was wrapped in cotton wool for six months and had leeches on her heart, she also had very bad varicose veins but lived till nearly seventy-seven.

I was now working at Yates & Co Dyers and Cleaners and was in the needlework department and enjoyed it; it was miscellaneous work, taking linings and fur collars out of coats and replacing after dying, unpicking bows and trimmings from wedding dresses to be dyed and again replaced, unpicking babies' cots for the covers to be washed and pram canopies, repairing jackets and trousers and also invisible mending, a special process which you had to learn.

I now had a long walk across the Downs, very bracing on a windy and snowy morning. To think I would walk home through the Downs on a foggy night and not be afraid.

After a few years I worked at a dressmakers opposite where we lived. We had an hour lunch break and half an hour for tea-break, both of which I came home for. Dad worked round the corner so neither of us had a journey, indeed I have never had to travel to business so must have saved myself a good deal of frustration.

It was a Jewish firm and the governor stayed in the room all day and watched and timed every movement, this coupled with the fact that it became a standing occupation which I have never been able to do, having curvature of the spine like my mother, caused me to leave. If you were required to work overtime he would tap you on the shoulder and say, 'Seven o'clock.' No warning, regardless of the fact you might have made arrangements to go out. One of my friends cried when she knew I was leaving and the girls gave me a green pen and pencil set.

I then went to work in a firm that made dressing gowns and housecoats; they did lovely work, quilted gowns diamond stitched all over (not like they do nowadays), bed-jackets with the whole sleeve covered with maraboo trimming, ninon tea-gowns, nuns' veiling gowns with cartridge pleated sleeves. I enjoyed it very much and stayed till the firm amalgamated with another firm and after, altogether forty-one years. It was not very good pay in those days, although I was on piece-work and quick we did get a lot of slack time. Our worst paid job was this, to put a button on a bed-jacket, first to find the material then

Worthing 1935.

Eastbourne 1938 or 1939.

you took a wooden button mould, covered it with wadding then the material, twisted it round with sewing cotton, cut off the surplus material and stitched it on the jacket after measuring the exact position. For this you received one farthing (a quarter of an old penny), after a time they went up to a halfpenny. Thank goodness those days have long since gone and now in the textile trade you can earn very good money.

One day a friend of mine who was a cutter, cut her finger and they sent her to hospital, after she had been gone about half an hour I fainted.

I made several friends during my working life, they would come home to tea and sometimes we would go and see a play. I remember all Ivor Novello's plays, 'Dancing Years', 'Perchance to Dream' and 'King's Rhapsody'. I have always been fond of the theatre and cinemas when films were worth looking at, it puzzles me why they cannot make such lovely films today. In my early years Greta Garbo was my favourite, and then such actresses as Anna Neagle, Greer Garson, Deborah Kerr and many others. Ronald Colman and Greer Garson in 'Random Harvest', and 'Mrs Miniver' with Walter Pigeon, those were the days.

I seldom went out on my own, my mother loved me with a possessive love, until you have experienced it you have no idea what it is like. Everywhere I wanted to go my mother always came with me, my father's work took him out all evening and she didn't like being left on her own.

One might ask, Why did I put up with it? but I am a moral coward and wanted to keep the peace, anyway I liked my home, what one might call a 'Home Bird' like my father. The three of us used to go on holiday to Worthing, Eastbourne and Cliftonville and also to visit dad's cousins at Ealing and mother's cousin at Esher.

Another War

1939 brought another war so very much worse than the last one, it was certainly brought home to us. The previous year, when war was threatened, mother and I decided we would like to make some alterations in the home. Dad was one of those men who didn't like change or even improvements but mum and I did, so after a general discussion for and against we got our way. I bought a sideboard, bureau and dining room suite and new curtains. My father was against this for two reasons, firstly he didn't like new things and secondly what a silly time to buy anything when we are expecting a war, he was right of course. Anyway, we were fortunate in not having our home destroyed like so many people.

To coin a much used phrase 'The day war broke out', the siren went just after eleven o'clock. My mother said, 'The artful things, they must have been on their way!' Of course it was a false alarm. There was one incident that was not funny at the time but we had a laugh about it after: the lady in the flat above us was very superstitious and would not normally pass you on the stairs, however, when the warning went I was running up and she was running down.

We had an Anderson shelter in the garden but we didn't use it much and we were fortunate in being able to sleep in the Star Laundry shelter, they had a purpose built shelter for their workers in the day time, as the working area had a glass roof. It was built in four sections, we kept our bedding there and slept there for five years. My father was then on night work. One section was for Mr and Mrs Smith, the governor and his wife and their maid, another for the chief engineer and his family, one for Smith's neighbours and the remaining one for mother and me. We used to go round about 9.30 and come home about 7 o'clock in the morning as it was only round the corner from our house.

One night we were on our way round when a bomb dropped in the next road in a school playground opposite where I worked. The caretaker, who had just lost his wife, and his daughter who was staying there and was pregnant were killed. Three houses in front of the firm were demolished. I didn't sleep that night thinking of the children and people in those houses, the next morning when we arrived at work we didn't know where to start clearing up the debris. Once again we were fortunate and people were amazed that we were not hurt. I saw what looked like a pencil flying through the sky then it seemed as if the building moved and hot cinders were falling down. When the raid was over we went home to see what damage had been done, everywhere was covered in glass, another minute and we would have been coming down our stairs and been cut to pieces. The windows were all blown out as they were on several occasions and mother's bedroom curtains were hanging down.

Once again God spared us.

One Egg

During the early days of the war we heard about the food situation in Germany which said they were only allotted one egg a week. I said, 'How can you manage on one egg a week?' little thinking that in the near future there would be many weeks when we wouldn't have any. Our ration was mostly 2 oz of everything. 1/6 worth of sweets per month, very short of sugar, a real handicap for us as we were sweet-toothed, we used saccharine tablets same as mother used in the first war. I still use sweeteners as I have lately given up sugar in my tea as I am rather overweight, though I was always well covered and as a baby my mother always had to buy clothes for an older child. My mother made our hairdresser laugh one day, we as a family did not like a lot of fat on our meat and our butcher seemed to give us more than our share. She said all she got from him was sarcasm and fat. Soap too was a problem, my mother had some cousins in San José California and Hawaii, Edwin-de-Lacey and his niece Genevieve and he sent us some soap, but we couldn't make it lather.

He once came to England on a visit and came to see us. It was a lovely day with a flawless blue sky and we remarked on it, he replied it looked muddy.

He was a bachelor and a very nice person. When he died he remembered my mother in his will.

In the war years I used to do the washing on a Monday evening. Invariably we would have a raid and go down to the shelter, by the time we returned the water would be cold. It was worrying to have a perm as your hair curlers were attached to flex on a stand and you couldn't get up and run.

We had a land mine drop on the Downs just at the back of us, luckily it lodged in a tree. The next day they came to defuse it and we all had to leave our homes for a while. We had bombs drop all round us but thanks to God we were spared.

Women were being called up to do army work. This rather worried me and I got alopecia (bald spots on the head) caused by worry. I was always a worrier by nature, but was not called up as I was a key worker, being the only one on my job. When I went for an interview two clerks were guessing what people's jobs were, when I passed by one said to the other, 'Office'. I have often been thought to work in an office, once someone asked my mother if I was a school teacher, at least I must look as if I have some brains.

There was a friend at work, Jean, who was bombed out so we gathered all we could spare and give to her, she was very kind to us and once when there was a coal shortage she brought us two bags of coal. At last the war ended in 1945 and we tried to resume our normal lives to be able to sleep at home and have an uninterrupted rest.

Getting Back to Normal

During the war I used to do private work. People were very glad of this because we still had clothing coupons and clothes were in short supply. I shortened and lengthened coats and dresses and did repairs and alterations. Once a customer sent by post a parcel of six sheets to repair and turn sides to middles, she would normally have discarded them. I don't suppose young people today know what sides to middles mean but it was the custom in our time, and if you were a practical housewife to make things last. A sheet always begins to wear thin in the middle and each side has plenty of wear in it so you tore it down the centre and joined the sides together. Christmas time I used to make tea-cosies and other fancy articles for the girls where dad worked. I also made two patchwork quilts, one for mum and dad's bed and one for mine, being able to get pretty pieces of quilted silk and satin from our cutting room. I have always liked to be busy and have plenty to do, I cannot sit idle for long.

There are two episodes that come to mind as I write. Once I had a fancy for a small coffee table. Thinking it would be easy to make one and cheaper, I went one morning to Stoke Newington where there was a woodwork shop and told the man what I had in mind. He soon said, 'Oh! you want Queen Anne legs!' By the time I had got home with four Queen Anne legs and the top I was exhausted. My father said, 'What on earth made you do it?' but between us we made it up and had it for quite a few years.

Another time I fancied a divan bed, mine had wooden bars at the head and foot so one day I got the saw and removed the two posts at the foot and 'hey presto', a divan bed. I didn't realize how hard this job was till I was half way through it. When my mother saw it she said it would look nice if I did the head as well but I said, no I have had enough. A few weeks later

Dad about 1951

We three.

I did it and bought some plywood and covered it with contact for a head board and was very pleased with the result.

We decided we would like an 'all night fire', they were fires you could bank up last thing at night and by turning a knob in the morning you would get a nice fire. I thought how nice, no more dirty grates, so we bought a tiled surround and the man came to fix it, first having to take out the old fireplace. While he was doing this the room looked rather like a London fog with all the soot flying about. After it was completed and we were told what to do, the next morning I turned the knob and waited and waited and not a glimmer, it was a miserable fire all day. In the evening my father was so cold he put on his overcoat, we found out after complaining at the shop they hadn't put sufficient earth at the back.

In 1952 we had a severe fog, they called it 'Smog' and said it was a killer. We had never had such a bad one before. I can remember some bad ones when young, one lasted seven days. 4,000 people died as a result of this and many more were made ill, everything was made dirty so it meant a lot of washing. This was the beginning of my father's illness, he got a cough and was generally ill then he contracted nephritis, a kidney complaint. He had never been ill in his life except for his ulcerated leg. He gave up work just three weeks before he died, aged seventy in the German hospital. A policeman came at 6.30 a.m. and told us he passed away in his sleep. That was the 10th December 1953. The doctors hadn't expected this and there had to be a post-mortem. If ever a man deserved heaven he did, I only wish he had had a few years without toil and trouble to relax as I am doing now.

My mother and I didn't know what to do with ourselves, especially being so close to Christmas, we had been such a united family. I spent the time sorting out his clothes and personal things, a most heartbreaking task, the sooner it was done the better. I just felt if only I could go to sleep over Christmas and wake up when it was all over.

To add to my misery just at that time there was a popular song called 'O Mein Papa'.

It took a long while for my mother to get over the loss, in fact I never thought she would, they were very happy and had been married forty-four years. Dad had been at his firm twenty-six years and had been presented with a Westminster chiming clock.

Now for something more cheerful, my father had a younger brother who was rather mischievous and one day he didn't want his mother to go out, so while she wasn't looking he put her hat up the chimney. I hope she had another because in those days it wasn't considered right to go out without one. On another occasion he had terrible toothache and my father took him to the dentist. When my father rang the bell he ran off leaving my father on the doorstep.

I have had three bad falls in my life so far, thank God without serious after effects. Once I was putting up the curtains and standing on a table and on getting down I must have put my foot on the side of the chair and went down with the chair on top of me. It could have been serious but my legs were both black with bruises. Another time I had not been feeling well and going to work on a Saturday morning decided to ride. I got one foot on the bus and the conductress rang the bell, consequently I was thrown in the road. It was a blessing there wasn't any oncoming traffic or I shouldn't have written this story, I was not hurt only shocked. On another occasion I put a pair of nylons on the corner of the bath and on passing must have knocked them on the floor, my foot slipped on them and I did a double somersault and cut my face just under the nose, it was bleeding rather a lot and I had to go to hospital. They said if it didn't stop they would have to put a stitch in it, they put a plaster on and gave me an injection. I was badly bruised, when I went to work one of the menfolk said, 'Who won?'.

Friends

Through doing private work I met some nice people from time to time and became friendly with a family named Price who were Quakers. Some time after Mrs Price died and we went to the funeral. It was conducted very differently from ours, first of all they bury the person then all the mourners go into the Friends Meeting House. Everything is very plain and austere, nothing is said for quite a while then suddenly someone will get up and start speaking about the deceased, then another and so on. After a long silence when it appears nobody has anything more to say everyone partakes of tea and cakes, they do not have any flowers.

Soon after Mr Price and his cousin made their home together so she could look after him and they bought a house at Gidea Park, we sometimes went there weekends and I kept friends with her till she died.

Some other people I met were Jewish, the sister of the one

who sent me a parcel of sheets during the war, she couldn't use her fingers properly and was glad for me to do any needlework for her. She died some years later, her husband had been very good to her, I used to meet him sometimes on a Saturday morning while out shopping. One morning he said, 'Would you get married?' I was pleased to say at that time no I couldn't, while my mother was still alive. She was then about eighty-four. I have been to two Jewish weddings so know a little about other people's religions.

Being an only child, also my mother, we seem to have drifted away from dad's family with the exception of his cousins who lived at Ealing. There was Uncle George and Aunt Emma, their son Ernie and daughter Ethel, and we have visited each other all through the years right up till the present day. The older ones have passed on of course, but we still keep in touch, sometimes only a Christmas card but nevertheless I am still in contact with Muriel, Ernest and Mavis who are all married happily and have their own families.

It appears many people don't remember it but we had an earth tremor one Saturday morning. I cannot recall the actual year, it must have been in the 1930s but my chair moved, a very uncanny feeling. Some people's crockery on the dresser fell off. Thank goodness we don't have such awful disasters like other countries, although an earthquake was reported from Colchester in 1884 and one person was killed. In 1947 and again 1963 we had very severe winters, said to be the worst in living memory, with snow piled high up the edge of the pavements.

There were about three girls I was extra friendly with at work who used to come home to tea. One was Amy, she came to the firm in 1940 after years at home looking after her mother, I first remember her when she came over to me one day and showed me some photos of one of her nephews' wedding. She has been a good influence in my life, she was a Congregationalist she also introduced me to Spiritualism, not that I am a spiritualist but when you are confronted with a medium and he tells you things that only you know about there is no disputing it. I once went to see a Mr Benjamin soon after I had lost my father. As he came into the room he said 'Who is William Scott?' I replied. 'He is my father.' He said he was at peace and happy, he could see him with a dog, we never kept one but he used to take out his governor's, and he could see him laughing about a moustache. Well, when my parents were on their honeymoon my father tried to grow a moustache but it wouldn't grow in the centre and he laughed about it and gave up. The medium also said he was gifted, well he was with his painting considering he never had a lesson.

About me he said I would have long life, I had no cancer or tuberculosis in me but would have severe rheumatism. I would move and be happy in the future, was clean and had a good hand and had healing powers in my hands, but I did not drink enough. There was no evil in my family. He ended up by saying my last days would be by the sea and I would not die in a hospital bed but my end would be sudden. Only those who live after me will know if this is true, much of what he said up till the present time is true.

Many years after I saw him he foretold the Moorgate tube disaster. One mystery remains, both he and another medium have told me I have a younger brother, they were very emphatic about it. This is strange as I am an only child and my mother never even had a miscarriage, funnily enough I have never regretted being an only child but always said if anything I would not mind having a brother.

Perhaps one shouldn't probe into the future, a lot of people don't agree with it but must say it has brought me a lot of comfort.

Although like my father's family in looks I am very like my mother in many ways, we are both rather emotional in a quiet way. A sad story or song will bring tears to my eyes such as 'Land of Hope and Glory', or seeing a Chelsea Pensioner on television.

We would often be thinking the same thing at the same time and we were both fond of writing, in fact I have inherited several things from my forebears: from my maternal grandpa, the love of buying and to be well stocked, from grandma tidiness and being thrifty, artistic like my father and Aunty Alie and being a bit cowardly when it comes to having to stand up for myself, and if I have a little streak of snobbishness in me, I know where that came from, my grandma's family.

Going from one thing to another, my mother and I and also my grandma, we all stuttered when young, it was in the Eggleton family. If I was sent on an errand as a child it was agony, certain words I could not utter, I always felt sympathy for our King George VI, when he was trying to make a speech. Luckily we all grew out of it as we matured.

As to my likes and dislikes, I have always liked running a home and all that it entails, washing, washing-up, ironing and shopping, I am not very fond of cooking and keep to plain dishes. I like writing, reading and having plenty to do, I think I must be a bit of a workaholic, a new word that has come into our modern vocabulary. I was always pleased to work overtime when asked and often brought work home. I like a busy atmosphere around me, to live in a busy street rather than a quiet one, houses and shops occupied rather than being empty and dilapidated. I don't like shortening of names and bad manners.

One very bad winter we had a burst pipe, there was water everywhere. On one occasion the people next door had to come to us for their water, one was a very nice young man called Norman, they lived in the top flat and had just got their first baby Sally. Evelyn, his wife, asked my mother to go in and have a cup of tea one afternoon and from then on became firm

1963 Evelyn, Norman, Sally and Susan in their garden.

friends. After a while they moved to Thorton Heath, Surrey, and we spent their first Christmas with them and they made us very welcome. I had seen them previous to our meeting going shopping arm-in-arm along Dalston Lane and thought they looked a nice couple.

About this time I bought our first television set. My mother was very lonely, at times unable to get about much so I thought it would be nice for her but knew I wouldn't have much time to look at it.

The first day when I got home she was looking fascinated at a TT motor race, normally she was not interested in sport any more than I am. I often think how my father would have liked some of the programmes like Peter Scott's nature series. The set was a Ferguson and caused us a lot of trouble and was always going wrong.

42

My mother who normally did the shopping because she liked to be out had to give up as it became too much for her, she had also put on weight, nearly twelve stones. When she was young she had what they called (salt cellars) hollows in the neck and a 17 inch waist, in those days it was fashionable to have a small waist and mother being a fashion conscious person tightened herself in so much that one day she fainted. In latter years when I measured her for a dress I had a job to find her waist.

I urged her to give up shopping because it was a worry to me to know she couldn't see properly. She said, 'What am I going to do for air?' Our friend Amy said, 'Open the window and look out.'

For a few years I became irritable and sometimes things seemed to get on top of me. One problem was our holiday, she couldn't get on a coach because being short the step was too high and she was stiff with arthritis so a colleague at work recommended a friend of hers who had a car and would take us to Worthing, and bring us back. We did this for two or three years and we also went to Gidea Park and Leigh-on-Sea to see our friends. He was very good to us in other ways and did a lot of jobs, he put mini castors on some of our furniture including a bedroom suite I bought for my mother, it made our furniture easier to move.

I managed to hire an invalid chair from the Red Cross while on holiday and also at home so we could go shopping. At that time on holiday we had a flatlet and did our own catering. I enjoyed it, we were often the first out in the house and the last ones in.

In latter years her life wasn't much pleasure, not being able to walk about and she couldn't see to read or sew. I had to leave her to go to business but she accepted her disabilities very well considering she was impatient when young, she had mellowed and had lost her temper.

Worthing 1959.

Moving

My mother now started to worry about me and realized that when she died I could be asked to move. The Star Laundry Company had sold our two houses to a private landlord, I don't think they would have actually turned me out but the rent book could not be held by a third person, so after dad then mother, I was the third and could have been in an awkward position. Hearing that a neighbour had moved into Navarino Mansions we decided to get my name on the list. I explained I wouldn't require it for maybe a few years but would need it later on. A friend whom I worked with, Edie Levy, lived there and she gave me a recommendation. Whether they misunderstood my letter or not I don't know but about a year after I was told to view a flat and only had an hour to decide. I didn't want to uproot mother at her age but we talked it over and decided to take it, my mother was game. We did want a two bedroomed flat but they wouldn't grant it.

Well from then on it was all go, first I got in touch with our decorator who had only done up our flat and hall and staircase two years ago. He had a small van and he and his wife took mother and me and a chair for her to sit on while we viewed the flat and decided about decorations. The electricity wasn't on so we had candles and torches. It was on the ground floor, neither of them said much and I could see they weren't very impressed. When we got home mother said, 'What a dump!' My heart sank in my boots and I thought, what have I done? I took another friend round from work and she said, 'You will make it look alright!'

I never slept properly for a week, all I could think of was wallpapers, curtains and multifarious things. We were blessed with three very good men, although we paid them I don't know what we would have done without them, they went out of their way to help us. First our decorator did up the whole flat, then we had an insurance agent who was more like a friend who was also an electrician, he did all our points and lights and put up a wall heater in the bathroom, then Frank who worked at a furniture store, (the one who took us on holidays) made our pelmets and helped me put up the curtains and did several odd jobs. We had new lino on all the floors and I asked a friend Alan at work if he would bring our carpets round in his van so everything went smoothly for moving day the 25th November 1966. But how to get mother there? It was arranged for the move to start at 8.30 so Lily, a friend at work phoned for a taxi to call for us at 8 o'clock which it did and the moving men came at the same time. I took mother in the taxi, sat her on a chair, put on an electric fire and left her to go back and see to the moving. The men came to disconnect the gas and electric, only one thing went wrong, the moving men forgot the kitchen cabinet which they went back for. I unpacked the tea-chests so they could take them away and everything was fine and it was a happy day. I had previously taken round a lot of small things so when we were there had clock, ornaments and New Home cards on the mantelpiece.

It was a blessing we did move because being all on a level it was a great help to mother. We liked the flat, as I still do, but not the outside surroundings, but you cannot have everything in life.

We had for some time the hairdresser Winnie and the chiropodist to come home to her.

A Parting

By now mother's health was deteriorating. One night she became unconscious so I left her sitting in the armchair while I went round to the doctor's. She said she couldn't come (it was only five minutes away) so she phoned for a duty doctor, he came about eleven o'clock and said her blood pressure was low. We had a specialist to see her and he said she should be in

Worthing 1959.

hospital. I didn't wish this and said I could manage but he said it was best. She was there eleven days, at the last she had a fall, she tried to get out of bed to go to the toilet and when I went to see her I had a shock, her face was bruised and black down one side. The last evening I saw her she must have been thinking of years gone by, she threw up her hands and said, 'Mummy, Mummy, I'm frightened!' These were very miserable days for me. At 7.30 a.m. on the first of May 1968 a policeman came to tell me she had passed away. I was not surprised, in fact I said to him, 'I know what you have come to tell me.' She was getting on for eighty-seven, the hospital said she had an enlarged heart. Very often at that age people are weary and tired and death can be kind.

The first thing I did was phone Evelyn and Norman. He came during the morning, after I had been to the hospital, and we went out and made all the arrangements, Town Hall for death certificates, undertakers and insurance offices, that was a great help to me. She was cremated at Finchley Cemetery.

As soon as mother went into hospital I returned to work. I had been home for six months to look after her. She had a life long friend Rhoda, they used to go to Sunday School together, strange to say she died three weeks after and I went to her funeral. I should never have gone, it was a sort of delayed reaction, I couldn't stop crying and had to leave during the service. Also another friend, Hannah, died during that year.

My mother had a cousin, Genevieve who lived in California and we had always corresponded. She had been presented at Court when she was young, I have a lovely photo of her when she was twenty-one. She also died a few months after my mother. She left money to mother so now it came to me, I have a copy of her will and it is most interesting to read.

She owned orchards of peaches, apricots and prunes and sometimes sent us a box containing eight or ten packets marked 'Sunsweet'. I have seen them in some of our shops.

A New Life

I was now on my own, but did not mind living on my own and didn't feel lonely. I had my work and then my firm moved to Clapton Ponds so now I stayed to lunch. Another friend at work, Ivy, said I needed a holiday so we booked a week at the Methodist Guest House at Bournemouth and later on a three day tour to Scotland.

I went out whenever the opportunity arose, to Norman and

Sally's confirmation, and to the cinema. I hadn't been for years but films were not like they used to be, I also went to the Zoo and Madame Tussaud's.

I now thought I would like to go to church regularly so tried one or two. Our old church at Islington had been pulled down to make room for flats so I went to the Central Hall, Mare Street, Methodist, and liked this best. They say it is a small world, I met Doris, a young although not so young now, woman that I worked with at Yates & Sons, the Dyers and Cleaners. She used to work in the despatch department over thirty years ago. That was not all, she said, 'Let me introduce you to my husband,' and who should he be but a man I met every morning and lunch-time going back and forward to work, we both looked at one another and laughed.

I soon got busy with bazaars and they let me have my own stall for aprons for Christmas and the Summer Fayre. When I retired I joined the Monday afternoon Sisterhood when we have prayers, hymns and a speaker. I have also taken over the birthdays, we send a card to all the ladies who come on Monday and now I keep the register for the offertory envelopes and issue them out, and go to the meetings for Women's Work and help on the stall. As regards religion it requires a lot of understanding, we are sure there is a God above but I do ask myself why does He allow such terrible things to happen. I have heard many replies to this question but am still curious. The first two winters after my mother died I had influenza, the first time just before Christmas, the following year just after. One year it was bordering on to pleurisy and I felt so ill I only wanted to die and kept thinking, I wonder who will find me? But I recovered and got back to my old self, then had a bad spell of giddiness and what I now know to be prostrate hyper tension which turned out to be blood-pressure. That type of dizziness which some of my friends have experienced is frightening till you know what it is. As you lie down and put your head on the pillow it is just as if the bed is whirling around and you hang on to it.

After a few years I wanted part of my flat re-decorated and as I had some dampness round the lower part of the walls, I spoke to the Superintendent about it. After inspecting it he told me I would have to move out while they treated it, this was a great surprise to me. They found me another flat, No. 62, strange to say that was my age at the time. The porters helped me in with the lino and carpets and I spent all one weekend doing the floors. I got someone to move me and when the gas fitters came to transfer the cooker there was no gas pipe in the new flat, only the meter, so for £3 they took mine out and put it in the new flat. I was soon straight and was there for fourteen weeks, I could have stayed there but preferred to return to my other flat. They replastered all the walls and re-decorated it fully, they also took out the fireplaces, they must have employed inexperienced men for the paper was sodden with paste and was a mass of wrinkles so it all had to come off. This was put right and I chose another lot of wallpapers. I bought a surround so was now able to have a nice picture over my fire, a Constable print of Flatford Mill. Eventually it was ready to return to so I moved back again and bought a fitted carpet and three-piece suite and dining suite and sideboard. Norman came one evening and did a lot of jobs for me like bathroom fittings, mirrors and pictures etc. He also made me a cabinet to put over my sewing-machine which is very nice and well made. Although as I have said I like moving, having two moves in fourteen weeks was a bit much, especially as I was not feeling too good.

My neck was getting more and more stiff as time went on. Olive a friend at business was the first to notice it and asked me if I had a stiff neck. I got a letter from my doctor to go to St Leonard's and after many X-rays and heat treatment he said it was arthritis and gave me a collar and said I would have to live with it. I gradually got worse and my doctor gave me a letter for the Royal National Orthopaedic Hospital in Great Portland Street. I went for treatment twice a week but it did not improve, only got worse, it was misery to do anything even ordinary jobs like washing up and washing and ironing, I was so fixed. To go shopping it was such a struggle to put the goods in my bag, my head would keep turning to the right. I used to long for it to rain when I went out so I could put an umbrella up and hide my head. I tried healing sessions at Balls Pond Road and Dawns Park Road (laying on of hands) that didn't help either, once I went to their headquarters in Belgrave Square, all to no avail.

By this time work was getting impossible and I had to give up. I had made up my mind to work till I was sixty-five or till I found it too much for me, it was a nice sitting down job doing what I liked at reasonable money and only working mornings if a bit hectic at times like all work places. One morning I said to the manageress I could not do any more so that was how I retired.

On my next visit to hospital they suggested I go into the Orthopaedic Hospital at Stanmore. Professor Thomas said the reason for sending me there was I would be admitted sooner than in London, I was to have retraction and bed rest. My first time in hospital, how I had always dreaded them but I felt so ill I couldn't get there fast enough. One humorous incident, they sent me a form to fill in to save time at the reception desk, one question puzzled me. 'Surname at birth' other previous surnames, I still cannot think what surnames you could have before you were born. I went in on the 15th July, a two and a half hour journey on three buses. Elsie Groom offered to come with me and I have always been grateful for the offer but being independent as always said I could manage. I went to the Admission Office in the grounds and after giving all particulars was told to take a seat and wait for transport. When it came it put me in mind of a horse box, it was so huge. I arrived in Zachary Merton Ward, undressed and got into bed. During the afternoon the sister and two nurses brought an appliance that fitted on my head with weights hanging down the back of the bed. I couldn't move so realized this was what meant by retraction. I couldn't sleep lying on my back, I also wondered why there was a mirror over the bed but was soon to find out. When breakfast time came I couldn't feed myself, you were supposed to balance the plate on your chest and look in the mirror. I just couldn't cope with this, once someone's visitor took pity on me and fed me.

After the second day they realized this wasn't going to work and removed it just before lunch, fish and chips were on the menu, I don't think I have ever enjoyed a meal more I was so hungry. I never got out of bed for three weeks, only to have a bath when they wheeled the bed into the bathroom and put me in it, washed my hair first then had the bath, other times they gave me a blanket bath. They gave me Librium and Valium. Taking these drugs I was very dopey, I couldn't write legibly and after three weeks when I got up couldn't walk straight. Amy came to see me several times and I didn't know what day it was.

After that they tried ice packs and I also had manipulation under anaesthetic twice. Later I went to group therapy, each person doing a different job to see how they could manage it. One man on two sticks made the tea, they asked me to make a cake and another time to wash up, what an ordeal.

One day coming back to the ward there was a lovely basket of fresh fruit from Harrods that my governor sent me. Being all that way out, I didn't expect many visitors but had plenty.

Amy came on Saturdays and one of the girls from business, Ella, brought Olive, Lily and Ivy in her car. Other visitors were Mr Healy and Ivy Lane from the church, Elsie Taylor and Grace Smith, Elsie Groom and Ivy Mitchell, Marjorie Slade who lives in my flats, Norman and Sally, and also one of my governors who lives at Stanmore.

I had about 25 Get Well cards and letters, it is surprising how this all bucks you up, the kindness of friends. It was a very nice hospital, they had carpet squares on all the floors and each patient had their own locker at the end of the ward to hang their clothes. There were very large grounds which I never walked through, it being difficult to walk as my head kept turning to one side, there was also a hairdressing shop in the grounds which was handy.

There was a church in the grounds which I went to twice, also a minister used to come Friday evenings to give the sacrament to anyone who would like it but only another young girl and myself took it, he did not have bread and wine but a small wafer.

On one occasion they sent me to a specialist and she asked me what were my parents' temperaments.

I was there for six weeks and my departure was sudden. It was the Friday morning before the August holiday weekend and they wanted to send as many patients home as possible so I was suddenly told I could go home. The other patients were sorry I was going because I was the only mobile one to answer the telephone. Anyway they advised me to stay and have my lunch first so I packed my things, having more than I took in, owing to presents friends had brought me.

I rang for a taxi to take me part of the way then got on two buses with all my things. I felt no better than when I went in. I took another taxi to my door and arrived home about four o'clock to an empty flat and no food, so went over to my neighbour Edie who was always ready to do a kindness and she got me just the bare necessities. My stay in hospital was an experience, for the most part pleasant, the three weeks in bed did me more good than anything, I have never had such a rest. They were mostly young patients and despite what they went through were always cheerful.

In one part of the ward there were young patients strapped to what they called a Stryker Frame, rather like an ironing board which revolved the person, being face upwards some of the time then face downwards.

On my next visit to Great Portland Street again I saw Professor Thomas and had more tests and X rays (have had 14 in all). He asked me to go to the Royal Free Hospital at Belsize Park, Hampstead, a modern hospital for an EEG test, this is an electrical device attached to the head with small rubber plugs and makes one's hair in an awful state. The result of all this is they considered they had sent me to the wrong hospital (Stanmore) and would I now go to the University College Hospital. They tried me on various tablets and at last a cure – a capsule, Halopheridal, in two shades of green. After a couple of weeks I could control my neck, I felt a different person and felt life was worth living. I lost $1^1/_2$ stones. I am grateful to all those doctors and nurses in all six hospitals who did their best to help me and all those who have prayed for me.

A Little Bit of Pleasure

I go to visit my firm sometimes to see my colleagues but it is lovely being at home to be able to relax after a working life with its stresses and strains.

I belong to the library and keep in touch with my friends, do jigsaws, make aprons for our bazaar, and sometimes children's clothes for the Shaftesbury Society.

I don't mind living on my own, I have got peace of mind which is worth a lot, most of my life seems to have been working against the clock. I am not tense like I used to be everything in the home is so much easier to run, not like the drudgery it was, I get through my work quickly although am particular, especially where food is concerned, when you think of how many hands it has gone through before you get it.

I have never smoked a cigarette, don't drink, only indulge in a sherry to celebrate someone's happy event, or a dose of hot whisky in bed if I feel a cold coming on. Which reminds me of an incident when I was in my young teens. Where I worked they had a Christmas party and I must have had too many ports for I went upstairs where someone had some calendars to sell and felt very generous and wanted to buy one for everybody. I never remember coming down those stairs.

Sometimes they have celebrities at our Town Hall and I have seen Sheila Scott the airwoman, Mrs Mary Wilson reading poetry, wife of the Prime Minister, and Godfrey Winn and Sybil Thorndike for whom there was a standing ovation. A few years ago we had two dances there. I have seen many plays but not lately, they are getting like the films with their blasphemy. I enjoy a good many things on television, 'Crossroads', 'Coronation Street', 'Emmerdale Farm', Quiz programmes, 'Holidays', 'Songs of Praise', 'Terry and June', 'Mr and Mrs', Arthur Negus and many others and Val Doonican, he seems so at ease, one song he sang I thought very moving,

'If you are the father of sons you worry,

If you are the father of daughters you pray,

Remembering you were once a boy.'

Moira Anderson is one of my favourites, not forgetting 'Hinge and Bracket'. There are many programmes that are crude with double meanings to ordinary everyday words, one has to think before one speaks.

Holidays

I have had some lovely holidays and been with several different friends. With Amy I went to Scotland, Devon and Cornwall, Newquay, Falmouth, Shanklin and Jersey, they were tours and most enjoyable. We flew to Jersey and went in a cable car, yet I cannot face an escalator. We have seen some lovely country and the scenery in Scotland is breathtaking, also Llandudno with its little railway and the Great Orme and Little Orme. One weekend we went to Blackpool just to see the illuminations and have had holidays in Bournemouth, Folkestone and my beloved

Worthing which is a place where I should like to live having been there on and off all my life.

I have also had several days out visiting stately homes and once while at Southampton we went over the *Queen Elizabeth II*.

I exchange visits with Evelyn and Norman and their three lovely daughters, Sally, Susan and Sarah.

I may as well mention a few details about one holiday Amy and I had, it was a Wallace Arnold Tour to York and Scotland in May 1977 for eight days. We had booked the previous October, you needed to book early. It started on Tuesday and we had a car to take us to King's Cross, we next stopped at Kettering for lunch then on to York where we spent two nights. The following day was a free day so we went to York Minster which is very beautiful, visited the Castle Museum and walked through an olde worlde cobbled street. There is a wall round the city where you can walk and we sat in some pleasant gardens. Next morning, Thursday, we were off and stopped at Washington for coffee, then Newcastle and Dunbar for lunch at the Royal Mackintosh Hotel, on to Callander for tea and finally to the Royal Hotel at Tyndrum for two nights. We went for a walk after dinner and saw only one shop. The following day we drove to Oban and over Macdonald's Mill it was a lovely day, we had lunch at McTavish's Kitchen. At Oban there is McCaig Tower which resembles the Colosseum.

We then went on to Easdale, there is a bridge there that takes you over to the Isle of Seil, built in 1792. We went in to see an artist and poet C. John Taylor. There was a very quaint lady walking around who resembled Queen Victoria with a lace cap, she was a nun.

On Saturday morning at 9 o'clock we started to make our way to Aberdeen, having coffee at the Croix Hotel at Fort William. One of the highlights of the tour as far as I was concerned was Braemar. I was looking forward to going into Crathie Church. Just before twelve we arrived outside but the Queen Mother was at the service and the police would not permit our coach to stop so we were disappointed. Also we could not go to Balmoral Castle because the Queen Mother was in residence. The mountain views are breathtaking, we went up one in the coach and some of the party got out and threw snowballs, we were 2,187 feet above sea level. Our next port of call was Perth where we had lunch at the Salutation Hotel, the oldest hotel in Scotland, built 1699, where Bonnie Prince Charlie stayed. Our last night we spent at Wells' Hotel at Shap Fell, this was a very isolated part but very picturesque.

Our fellow passengers were pleasant company and we sat at table with two nice ladies who were mothers-in-law, one's son having married the other's daughter. The weather was lovely, so were the hotels, some had electric kettles in the bedrooms where you could make your own tea. When in Edinburgh we drove through Princes Street. Coming home we had lunch in Staffordshire and arrived at King's Cross just after six when we phoned for our car. We had driven 1,700 miles, all very interesting, the brochure price was £73.50. In 1978 Amy and I went to Llandudno for another lovely holiday. I have two albums full of snaps and cards of all my holidays which I still enjoy looking through.

Shops and Cinemas

When I thought life was getting a bit uneventful something happened which gave me a new interest, a friend at business named Olive wanted to make a home of her own. After looking over two flats and deciding against them she bought a maisonette at Leyton, she has had it modernized and it now looks very nice. We got busy choosing curtains, carpets and furniture and everything needed for the home and I made the curtains and enjoyed it all. I have known Olive for years and been friends but we have now got closer and we keep in touch with phone calls and visits. What a boon the telephone is, I only wish I had had it years ago, it would have been so handy when my mother was alive. I always thought the phone was a means of keeping in touch with friends especially when you are a distance from one another but some folk never think to give you a call.

Now we have a happy Jubilee year to look forward to. I saw the Queen and Prince Philip when they drove through Dalston Lane, same as I did the day after the Coronation in 1953, and some years ago I saw the Queen Mother looking at the children's flower beds in the grounds of Sigdon Road school which is opposite my old firm, she looked a picture in a pale mauve dress.

A few months ago our church took part in a 'Songs of Praise' service for television at our parish church of St John. This was very interesting, we had two sessions of two hours each for a rehearsal before the actual recording.

On the 9th of December 1979 I had a nasty experience. It was nine o'clock on the Sunday evening, I was coming home from a visit to Evelyn and Norman's. A youth must have followed me when I got off the bus and just outside my entrance he was right behind me, he said, 'Give me your handbag, right, give me your bag!' He had what looked like a knife pointing at me. I gave it to him and as soon as I got indoors rang 999 and the police came in a few minutes, and took me in a car round the Pembury corner where I recognized him. We all went to the station and he was questioned. I was told the case would be some time before it came up.

Fourteen months passed and I was not informed till 10 o'clock the night before that I was to go to the Old Bailey. I went with a Detective Constable in a taxi and after a long wait was called to the witness box and sworn in. The case took a day and a half and the jury were out an hour, the result, 'Not Guilty'. So that was the end of that, but I was relieved when it was over because for those fourteen months I never knew from one day to another, even on holiday, when I would be summoned.

I suppose in these days I should be grateful to him, at least he didn't attack me as so many of them do today, not satisfied with robbing you they take a delight in battering you to death, especially old people who have only got their pension. People were poor years ago and there was unemployment on a large scale but they didn't rob you. Now we have to be locked and bolted in and not many people care to go out after dark, I don't for one, and if I do see a friend and stay after dark I have a car home. In that respect the old days were the 'Good Old Days'. Today there is lack of respect, of common courtesy, a general don't care attitude here in London, there is quite a different mode of behaviour when we go on holiday. The other day while on a bus a young woman got on with a baby in her arms and a little child holding on to her skirt, there sat a young lad, when I offered her my seat he eventually got up. Thank goodness all our young people are not like that.

Our district has deteriorated like a lot of others, for one thing we have lost all our nice big shops. When we came to live here in 1930 Matthew Rose's was the leading store where Marks & Spencer's now stands in Mare Street then further down in the Narrow Way there was Parnell's, noted for lovely dress materials. On the corner of Clarence Road there was a cinema called the Clarence, and many shops including the International, with one big department store called Spokes. Mr Spokes was always seen to be wearing a buttonhole, in those days and before there would be a shop-walker who would show you to the department you wanted and offer you a chair. A very ingenious way of paying your bill was known as an overhead railway, the assistant would put the money and bill in a small wooden cup and screw it on to a metal holder, pull the handle and it sped along the wires to the cashier's office. She would remove money and enclose any change there might be replace cup, pull a handle and back it came to the customer. Most prices, whatever the amount, would end with $11^3/_4$ farthings, in the trade they thought it sounded cheaper than a whole shilling, like they do nowadays when goods are marked so many pounds and ninety-five pence.

If you bought from a small grocer's shop they generally weighed things while you waited, sugar for instance, they would make a cone shaped blue bag, and butter they would keep patting and returning it to the scales till it was the correct weight. Some shops seem to have disappeared, like oil shops and corn chandlers and now we have shops that we never had years ago such as DIY shops, charity shops, heels done while you wait, job centres and Building Societies, we have five in the Narrow Way. Years ago when I was a child, for those who know Stoke Newington Road, there was a large corner shop at Foulden Road where three or four men sat cross legged in the window doing tailoring, and from Stamford Hill to Dalston there were seven cinemas. If you didn't go early you would have to queue, the prices were 6d, 9d, 1/3 and 1/9, once when we went to see 'Sunnyside Up' with Janet Gaynor and Charles Farrell we had to pay 2/- (two shillings) and thought that very extravagant. One thing I forgot to mention we didn't have launderettes like we do today, where you wash your dirty linen in public.

We managed to enjoy ourselves in those days and some evenings would play games, Snap, Happy Families, Alma and Dominoes. The houses just past ours in Amhurst Road, had carriage drives and many people kept servants, all your shopping would be delivered to your door by errand boys on bicycles, and you wouldn't dream of going to church without a hat.

While I have been talking about shops in this chapter there is a funny little story I would like to tell. A mother asked her two young daughters to go to the butchers and get some belly of pork. Being rather shy and not liking to say the word 'belly' they asked the butcher if they could have some stomach of pork.

A good many years ago I came into a little money from a legacy so to celebrate I took my colleagues out for the evening to the Comedy theatre and saw 'Girl in my Soup' which turned out to be a disappointment. It was 1969, I have just looked at the programme (have a shoe box full very interesting things to look back upon), nevertheless we enjoyed our evening out, the prices, four seats (stalls) £6 four bus fares there and back 14/- four ices 7/6 and four programmes 4/- total cost £7.5.6. Now it would cost nearly double for seat alone. I have seen some very good plays in the past one in particular, 'Crown Matrimonial' at the Haymarket, a story of the abdication with Wendy Hiller taking the part of Queen Mary, as she came on the stage the audience gave a gasp at the resemblance. I have also enjoyed visits to Sadler's Wells.

1981 Happy Events

July 2nd brought news of the birth of Lucy to Sally and Christopher, eldest daughter of our friends Evelyn and Norman whose wedding I went to in August 1979.

Gladys and I had a nice holiday at Folkestone, weather rather chilly. We had booked for Wednesday 22nd–29th July but learning of the wedding of the Prince of Wales and Lady Diana we both wanted to see it on television so altered our holiday to the week before. Indeed it was a beautiful day and like most people I sat glued to my set, having an early lunch. When it was all over and they went on their honeymoon, I went out for a breath of fresh air. It was a tonic and a day to remember and they are a lovely couple, blessed with the love of a nation.

New Church Proposed

During this last year and after much discussion we are having a new church built. We are leaving our old premises because it's too large for present day needs and too expensive to keep up. So by demolishing four small shops they built a small church.

Small is the right word, the church itself is adequate but not sufficient room for bazaars and jumble sales and no room for a Sunday School, which is a very important item. Our minister, who had a lot of worry over this new project, reached retiring age and we were sorry to see him depart. September when the Methodist new year commences we welcomed Mr Peter Timms and family, a former prison governor, and our other minister Mr Glendinning. The Revd Timms we often see on television and hear on radio. The 3rd and 4th of April 1982 was the official opening of the new church, a very happy occasion, and a number of the old members came who had moved away. Our minister who had helped so much, Revd Healey, came and we were literally full up, having chairs in the vestibule. We went back to the Central Hall for refreshments and back again for a service in the new church, though small it is very cosy. We are supported much by our coloured community and there are several christenings but as most of our members are getting older there don't appear to be many younger ones to take their place. It is sad to relate but some people look upon you as an oddity if you attend a place of worship, they have no time for God.

I cannot help feeling if more of our children were brought up in a Christian environment there would not be the trouble with young people that there is today.

We have been fortunate in having nice ministers, men that you could talk to and are homely but each one of them has had trouble of some sort and tragedy in their private lives.

One day while on a bus I met one of our old members who left when she remarried, strange but she bears the same name as me, Edith Scott, I thought she would like to meet some old friends so arranged a tea party one Saturday, needless to say there was plenty to talk about and we all enjoyed ourselves. We have had several gatherings here, and sometimes about four or five of us meet on a Thursday afternoon and have a pleasant

Kathy and Edith.

natter, sometimes at Hilda's and Kathy's. I have now got a nice circle of friends at the church, not forgetting Margery Stead and Bobby and Gladys at the 'Limes', I nearly always go once a week and have a coffee where I always get a warm welcome.

Every year we have a coach outing, usually to Clacton, for the Sisterhood and Sunday School and pray for fine weather sometimes granted and sometimes not but we have been mostly lucky. We have two worthy gentlemen at our church who own cars, Mr Eddie Lane and Mr Alf Final who kindly give some of us lifts. September 1st brought another get together with tea and cakes with Hilda, Kathy, Irene, Marjorie and Beaty and Alf.

A friend that we all knew had been very ill for about five years, a diabetic, she was a member of the Round Chapel in Clapton but came to our church some Sunday mornings and to the Monday Sisterhood. I had known her and her mother for some years as she lived in these flats, her name was Marjorie Slade. Her health gradually deteriorated, twice she became unconscious and through Hilda seeing her light still on one morning we went round and the Superintendent got a ladder to get in the window, she was slumped in her chair unconscious. She was taken to hospital and put in intensive care.

When eventually she died we considered it a happy release, she had suffered enough, I am sure if it hadn't been for Hilda she wouldn't have lasted as long as she did. She gave five years unstinted service in getting shopping paying bills etc. and not always feeling well herself. The day she was cremated, her brother, nephew and five other friends including Hilda, Ivy Lane and Marjorie Final came back to me for sandwiches and tea and coffee and to my surprise stayed till 5 o'clock chatting happily.

A big surprise was on Sunday morning when Marjorie and Ivy gave me a lovely box of chocolates. A few of us helped to dispose of her belongings, Ivy, Hilda, myself and Beaty and Alf took a lot away in their car, I don't know what we would do without them when it comes to hauling things around for jumble sales and bazaars.

In September Amy and I went again to Worthing but it was marred by Amy having a fall downstairs in the night, I have never seen a face so bruised it was a terrible shock for her and even for me to look at it. We went to a chemist and he advised her to go to hospital which we did and they gave her some ointment to put in her eyes which were nearly closed. She took it all in her stride and we went out as usual. Having tea one day in a cafe I was conscious of a lady looking, so mentioned that my friend had a fall, she replied that she had thought, that poor soul, having to go about with that birthmark. On seeing Amy about three weeks after there wasn't a trace of a bruise, one lady at the hotel said, she was so sorry for her but couldn't look at her. It is a very nice place where we stay, perhaps it would not appeal to some folks as it is mainly a residential hotel for elderly people who all have their own room and each have a table to themselves in the dining room, a place where I would feel comfortable if I had to have a holiday on my own. After coming home that year I had a yearning to go and live there, say when I get old and decrepit and running a home is a chore, but the main drawback is you would miss all your friends. Amy has now become too feeble to go on holidays, in fact she is in 'Sunshine Lodge' in Leytonstone and I go and see her. Before she gave up her home I managed to get her a home help by writing to her doctor.

Out and About

Going back to winter 1981, which turned out to be a bad winter, just before Christmas, being nervous of walking in snow and ice because I am not sure footed, I stayed in ten days in succession. I could not get out to do my Christmas shopping (food) and did not have my usual Christmas dinner, chicken with all the trimmings but managed to find something in my larder which I always keep well stocked especially in winter months. I managed, but I blessed our milkman who brings round eggs and bread, like others he deserves a medal trudging on his round every day and always cheerful, he did say he had a cheap line going in sun tan oil.

Occasionally I go to Oxford Street and nearly always before Christmas to look at Selfridge's shop windows. I watched a programme on television about Selfridges, they opened in 1909 and now employ 3,000 staff and £3,000 a day is lost in shop lifting, their takings are between a quarter and half a million a day, incredible.

Another nice department store is Jones Bros of Holloway which opened in 1905 and is where Crippin bought three pairs of pyjamas.

I am sorry to say I do not know a great deal about London

when it comes to places of interest, I went to St James's Palace to see the Queen's presents for her Jubilee and have been on a Sight-Seeing bus.

Having never seen the changing of the guard at Buckingham Palace I went one day and not being quite sure of my way asked two ladies who I thought were going that way to direct me. They replied in an American accent, we walked along and chatted, that brought me down to size. It was a very cold and windy day and even the guardsmen had mittens. Leaning against the barrier you hardly heard a word of English, it was all foreigners with their cameras, but we were rewarded by seeing the Princess of Wales drive in, she smiled and waved.

I had to attend Moorfields in High Holborn, they put drops in my eyes and coming out into the street everything was so blurred I was rather afraid to cross the road, so next time I went Kathy came with me which was very kind of her. When another friend had to go I went with her in case she had the same experience. Like years ago when some of us took it in turns to take Mrs Couchman to St Leonards to visit her husband.

Another hospital visit was back to the University College Hospital who wanted to see me to know how I was, it was for research. It was seven years since my last visit with my neck trouble and I was happy to tell them there had been no recurrence of the trouble. Only a short time ago I found out what the tablets were for, (Haloperidol) that cured me, of all things schizophrenia and anxiety. The latter could be attributed to the stress of years ago. When I mentioned this the doctor said some drugs that are for a specific illness cure other complaints also, it is rather an unusual complaint and lasts about five years and he had had only forty people with it in the last ten years.

April 1982 brought the Falklands war with a heavy loss of young lives and heartbreak to their loved ones, if I had only one wish it would be 'No more wars here or anywhere else'.

I had a surprise visit from the eldest of my three third cousins, Muriel, and we did enjoy a chat, we usually only meet at weddings and funerals. She lives at Greenford, her brother at Northolt and younger sister Mavis at Ealing.

My first cousin Alice I have not seen or heard of since her father's funeral in 1935, it is a shame how some families drift apart. One thing, I would like to know about my forebears, I know as far back as my great grandparents on my mother's side but would like to go further back still. I have been to Somerset House with a friend who wanted to read a will but we were referred to St Catherine House.

More Holidays

About January or February I thought about booking holidays. Knowing Amy was unable to go, I thought of going on my own but discussing it with Olive we decided to go together. Telling this to Kathy I felt she might like to join us but on asking her she said no, she would feel she was intruding. I assured her she was welcome so she decided to come, so I booked three bedrooms with full board for September 11th at the Cumberland Hotel at Worthing, right on the front where I had been several times. A friend of Amy's, a Mr Elcock, had always taken us and he did this time. After I had booked the thought struck me had I done the right thing, not about us three getting on together, I had no doubt about that, but me being very fond of Worthing, wondered, they being both younger than me if they would like it as much. I need not have worried they enjoyed it immensely, we all had a lovely week and perfect weather.

We toured the shopping centre in the mornings, went to Debenham's for coffee, Kathy and Olive went paddling after lunch while I minded all the bags then had a cup of tea. I have some lovely snaps to put in my albums.

Two sad happenings that week, a church friend, George Cook, died suddenly and Princess Grace had a fatal car crash.

Edith, Margery and Kathy, 1985.

But apart from that we had a memorable happy holiday. Olive and Kathy kindly gave me a pretty pill-box. That was 1982 and we have been every year since but this year, 1985 Olive is unable to come and Margery Stead is coming. I might add that sometimes we do buy a lot, one year in particular, two winter coats, hat, a large picture, a bag of jigsaws, our ordinary coats and three bags of shopping that we do on Saturday morning for us to take home.

I have been to Folkestone several times with Gladys and twice her son and wife have taken us, they are a very nice family and the hotel we go to is very comfortable too and very good cuisine. At breakfast the waitress asked what we would like, bacon and egg, bacon, egg and tomato or if you have a good appetite, bacon, egg, tomato and sausage, what we call a 'Full House'. I have a fair appetite and enjoy my food so had a 'Full

House' from then on, this amused Gladys she said it sounded like Bingo.

Speaking of hotels and food reminds me of a little story I heard recently, of a couple who took her father out to dinner all very nice and select, but the father not being accustomed to such surroundings sort of let them down. The waiter offered the wine list but father was not interested and after a while turned and clicked his fingers to the waiter and called out, 'Oi! got any beer?'

Up to the time of writing I have been on holiday with eight different friends and have never had any unpleasantness.

A Mishap

Monday 29th November 1982 being a nice morning I made up my mind to go and look at some freezers, but coming home fell when I got off the bus. I cannot think how or why but my foot just went over, the pain in the ankle bone was severe. A young man standing at the bus stop helped me home. Thinking it was a sprain I put a cold water bandage on it, but by early evening it was so swollen I rang for the doctor. He came and gave me a letter for the hospital next morning and made arrangements for an ambulance. I had to be ready by 8.30 and there I sat till 11 o'clock. On arriving I had an X-ray then waited and waited, I eventually they took me to the technician to have a plaster put on, I had got a fractured ankle. They found me a pair of steel crutches then another long wait, a receptionist took pity on me and asked would I like a cup of tea which she brought and two slices of bread and butter, it was indeed welcome. I arrived home about 6.30, they carried me in and sat me in my armchair and said I must not put my foot to the ground. Only people who live on their own know what a predicament that is. I enquired if they could just keep me in one night but they said they didn't have a bed. The technician said that if my toes turned black or felt strange I was to ring immediately as I would lose my toes. Well you can guess how I felt when later that evening saw one of my toes very dark and numb so rang them up, they said if I could move it it could be left till tomorrow. As it turned out it was the bruise coming out. When I got there they removed all the plaster and put on another lot, I got home that day by 2.30 just by luck.

We were all waiting in wheelchairs, some with sticks in the reception area waiting to be taken home, one man a Mr Levy who was tired of waiting asked at the desk, if they were making the ambulance? After a while he left so I was able to take his place, it's an ill wind they say. Had to go again the following day for a spot check and arrived home by 4.30 but what a job to get about! I don't know what I would have done without the help of kind friends, Olive, Kathy, Hilda, Helen Hurley and Florrie, Daisy and Rene H all paid me a visit. I am usually independent but you cannot do without people, not liking to trouble folk I rang up for a Home Help just to do my shopping she came for three months and was a very nice person.

Being housebound over Christmas I could not of course go to Thornton Heath on Boxing Day as I usually do, but was quite contented, had plenty of food, the television, was not in any pain so counted my blessings. Friends are surprised at me not minding being indoors and alone but I am quite resigned to it. I am never bored or suffer depression, sort of feel an inner peace, tranquillity within one might say.

I needed a visit to the hairdressers and she kindly gave me a lift there and I got a mini-car home. One thing that does lower one's spirits I think is if one's hair does not look as nice as possible, which is not often in my case because it is problem hair. Ivy and Eddie were very kind in taking and bringing me home on three Sundays and Ivy for her frequent phone calls.

At last the great day came when the plaster was to come off, they X-rayed it first then removed it and it was alright. The next day was my birthday and it was a very happy one, you wouldn't believe what sheer joy it was to go shopping in the Narrow Way after being housebound for two months, also looking forward to the afternoon when Gladys, Florrie, Hilda and Kathy came to tea and Olive later on. Through this mishap I have got friendly with two of my neighbours, one who lent me several jigsaws and the other, Helen, who was very kind in getting my pension. We now meet once a week and have a cup of tea and a chat, indeed I have never had so many friends in for tea and coffee, lovely.

Springtime and A Wedding

Now we have the spring to look forward to apart from the lovely flowers and trees in blossom there are several notable events always at this time of year, 'Ideal Home Exhibition', Budget, 'Boat Race', 'Women's World Day of Prayer' and putting on the clocks. An easy way to remember is Spring Forward, Fall Back, and of course spring-cleaning which reminds me of a joke told to me by Ellen. A little boy said to the Vicar, 'Is that right that we come from dust?' 'Yes,' replied the vicar.' And do we go back to dust when we die?' 'Quite right my son,' replied the vicar. 'Well in that case,' said the boy, 'you had better look behind the organ, I don't now if they're coming or going.'

I had received an invitation for Easter Saturday 2nd April 1983 to the wedding of Susan, middle daughter of Evelyn and Norman. She was to be married, at their local church where they are members, to Alexisjohn Stafford, met him once and he seemed very nice. At one time he thought of entering the ministry.

I left home at 9.30 to make my way to Thornton Heath, left my bag at the hotel that I had previously booked for bed and breakfast (same as I do Boxing night). At 1 o'clock I left to go to the church for the 1.30 service.

It was a very pretty wedding and the church was full, beautifully decorated with flowers the bride had done herself, being a florist she is used to flower arranging. The service, music and choir were very nice, they sang three hymns, as the bride entered, 'All people that on Earth do Dwell', then after the address, 'Now thank we all our God', and after the marriage, 'O Jesus I have promised'. Susan wore a cream watered silk crinoline dress with small posies of tiny yellow roses caught here and there on the skirt, two bridesmaids in green slipper satin and dear little Lucy carrying a small basket of flowers. The whole colour scheme was pale yellow and green, Evelyn wore pale grey.

After it was all over we stood outside about 45 minutes while photos and snaps were taken, we all felt a bit cold as there was a keen wind blowing, but it was dry. We then made our way to the reception held at the Aerodrome Hotel, about eighty-seven guests to mingle and chat and have a glass of sherry. Then the Toastmaster asked us to make our way to our places at table, I was on table D there, were five tables. We commenced with a prawn cocktail, buttered roll, turkey, beef and ham with salad, fresh fruit and cream, two cups of coffee, After Eights, wine, champagne and wedding cake. The tables were decorated with small baskets of yellow flowers and emerald serviettes. Evelyn and Susan went to Covent Garden at five o'clock one morning to get the flowers.

The happy couple left for their honeymoon at 7.15, destination unknown, for a few days then on to Brittany.

Some of their friends got busy doing up their car with balloons and streamers. The bar was open for a while for guests to partake of what they wanted and as I was thirsty had two glasses of pineapple juice.

All in all it was a very nice wedding and all went off smoothly. It brought back memories of Sally's wedding to Christopher (13th October 1979) also a nice young man and an equally nice wedding. A few of us returned to Evelyn's home for a while, then I was taken to the hotel, went to bed early and slept, had breakfast next morning and then went to Evelyn's and Norman's for lunch, and after a cup of tea left and arrived home at 5.30 having spent a very happy Easter weekend.

Age

They say age creeps up on you, sometimes it takes large strides, twice the other week two ladies got up and gave me a seat on the bus, I expect I looked a bit weary for going out makes me very tired, especially if I have to carry anything. I do not get tired so much doing household jobs, but oh! going out, my feet ache. I was told they were deformed by arthritis so that may be the reason and I also have a job getting on a bus because my knees are stiff. When shopping I take my ever faithful shopping basket on wheels, bought it for my mother as she had the same trouble. Being a little overweight doesn't help, other than that I enjoy good health and a good night's sleep, so many people do not sleep well. I feel sorry for them because the hours do drag. I am very grateful for my good health, have had several visits to hospitals for small growths that come on my face from time to time but they are not cancerous. My time is fully occupied visiting friends, housebound or in hospital.

When seeing my doctor some time ago he asked me if I was working and when I said I was retired he said, 'Don't you get bored?'I have never been so happy in my life, what with seeing friends doing all my own jobs, making my clothes, doing odd jobs of sewing for people making aprons doing embroidery and jigsaws. I think he was surprised. I also belong to the library and usually read biographies, I have not had a bad life and have no regrets, may have missed out on the best thing in life, but have also missed the heartbreak that goes with it, widows and widowers. Didn't I see how my mother was, one thing I always admired her for she gave up a lot and theirs was a true love match.

When I was young I thought how nice to have four children, I am very fond of children, and cannot take my eyes off them when they are young and amusing. Mentioning this to a friend, she said she wanted six sons and what had she got, one daughter, and with children comes heartache too. Many parents get hurt over the thoughtlessness of their sons and daughters, when just a phone call would make all the difference. I have just watched the programme 'Nanny' on BBC1, what a nice series, and I also saw the story of Noel Coward. What a lot of good films were made from his writings, 'Cavalcade', 'Brief Encounter', 'In Which we Serve' and 'This Happy Breed' just to mention a few. The commercials don't bother me but I quite enjoy those children's adverts. A little girl we know, Michelle, was eating an ice one day but rather slowly so a friend said, you had better eat it quickly or else it will come out of your ears. Putting her hand up to her ears rather cautiously she suddenly said Oh! you're pulling my leg. A few days later looking at the boats on the river at Richmond she said, 'Look, the boats are swimming.'

On to television again, I listened to a very interesting discussion on 2 o'clock Plus interviewing young married couples, with Marjorie Proops who I think is a very nice person and has been happily married for forty-seven years. Although she doesn't have a lot in common with her husband she stresses how important it is to give and take and also to be able to respect one another.

A pleasant surprise on the programme 'Three Little Words' on 27th April was seeing our other minister and his wife, Mr and Mrs Glendinning, taking part. I am looking forward to seeing them again next week.

Going through some old papers I found an account about my grandfather who was a compositor, he worked on the *Westminster Gazette*, an evening paper, from its first issue, and was remembered for his organizing abilities and brightness of spirit and unique personality. He would go to our church before and after his work to help cope with the running of it.

Nowadays I do not have a newspaper but listen to the news three times a day on radio and television, years ago we had the *Daily Sketch* and the *People on Sunday*. In August our minister the Revd Peter Timms left which was rather sad, and I went to the farewell service on the Sunday evening. As I had been to Springfield Park in the afternoon I thought instead of going home then out again to church I would have a snack in the tearooms and then get a 253 bus to church. Not being sure of what time they closed, I popped in and asked the owner, what was the latest time he served tea? He thought for a moment then replied, about October. I laughed and said that I meant today. About 5.30 he said and not a smile passed across his face. It rather put me in mind of something similar that happened when I was a child, I was in the bakers with my mother, she usually had a loaf called a long tin. Being told they weren't up yet, she asked how long would they be, the baker stretched out his hands about a foot long. It is really funny how one's questions can be misinterpreted, but a little humour goes a long way to lighten the day. A humorous little story as told by Princess Anne when visiting a hospital in Australia: a nurse wanting to sympathise with her patient said, 'Now you haven't come in here to die.' 'No came the reply, I came in yester-die.'

We had a nice holiday this year, again going to Worthing, we are known now by the residents who sometimes refer to us as the 'Three Graces'. We had good weather except the Sunday morning, coming home from church we had a struggle fighting against the gale and beating rain, you couldn't hold up an umbrella. To our surprise Kathy said she wouldn't have missed it, I said I would. The first night of our stay, there was a body found on the beach opposite our hotel, we never heard any details. As mentioned before we tour the shops, maybe it is because we have more time to browse, we even bought some Christmas presents. We also viewed a Show Flat on the front all very nice but at £55,000 we were not tempted. One day when

My good neighbours Lou and Ernie May standing by the wall and Helen Hurley next to me (with dark coat and silk scarf).

they were short staffed in the dining room we asked if we could have some more toast, in her haste instead of saying brown or white she said, what colour?

One morning Kathy and I went to Harrods, actually my first visit. It was the day after Princess Anne opened the food hall, and there was a beautiful bowl of yellow roses all made in butter. I have paid several visits to Leadenhall Market which is very quaint.

I enjoy my weekly shopping, mainly Sainsbury's and Marks & Spencer's and like the supermarket style of shopping, just choosing what you want and being able to get a small amount of anything if so required. It must also be an asset for deaf people but of course a handicap for blind people. We have a young woman living in these flats who is deaf and dumb and can only see very little, her husband is also deaf and dumb, and she goes shopping, what courage. One day the pavement was being repaired and there were no workmen there and I happened to be walking a few yards behind her, so I automatically said, 'I'll take you along,' quite forgetting she couldn't hear me. As I took her arm she was so startled and probably thought someone was going to molest her, I felt helpless but she managed without mishap. One has only to walk in any street to see handicapped folk which make you count your blessings.

Dreams

As I have said I am fortunate in being a good sleeper, go to bed about 10 o'clock and have a read and wake up anytime between 6.30 and 8.30 but I do dream almost every night, generally about the house we lived in for thirty-six years in Amhurst Road and about the people who lived there, my parents and people I have worked with. The strange thing is in my dreams they are all mixed up with the friends I have today whom they had never met. One of our ministers said we should write down and make a note of all our dreams, in that case I shall have to start another book.

At my optician's recently he spoke about prices, said he was doing a survey on the cost of spectacles today and years ago in relation to people's earnings and did I know what my earnings were years ago? He asked the right person because I have kept a record of earnings and what clothes etc. cost, for example in 1931 I bought a very nice bottle green winter coat with a marmot fur collar price three guineas, £3.3.0 in old money. Now you couldn't get much of a coat for less than seventy or eighty pounds. A pair of shoes for 12/11. My first pair of glasses in 1936 were £1.7.0 in 1983 £57 and I could go on and on.

In 1983 I had a nice holiday with Gladys again at Folkestone. Her son Peter and his wife Jean took us in their car and we made an early start, were called for at 7 o'clock and arrived there just before nine, all that way in 1 hr 50 min, takes me longer than that to go to Thornton Heath by bus. I think the proprietor was rather taken by surprise, he was only expecting two people about eleven o'clock and seven walked in at nine, for Peter and Jean had brought their daughter and her two children for the ride, they all wanted something to eat as they hadn't stopped for breakfast so asked for bacon sandwiches. We had a nice week and while there saw an air display by the Red Devils.

Just before Christmas a bomb went off at Harrods killing five people and many injured on a Saturday at 1.30, the most busy period when people were doing their Christmas shopping. How can people be so wicked? Now we are approaching 1984 this year has simply flown, I wish time would stand still for a while.

We have had our share of strikes, DHSS, pension books, eleven weeks without *Radio Times* and for the best part of the year the miners strike, with all the misery, hardship and bloodshed between police and pickets in those towns setting father against son and neighbour against neighbour. In the end we have all got to pay for it. On the 8th May the Queen opened the Thames Barrier, a wonderful piece of engineering. In May we had our Easter Offering stall and took nearly £40.

This same year, 1984, Gladys and I went to Bognor (a council holiday) and Alf Final kindly took us to the coach, a nice holiday but Gladys wasn't well enough to enjoy it and three days after we came home she was in hospital, but soon recovered and was her happy cheerful self again. She has a lovely disposition and makes everyone welcome.

While at Bognor there were two gents talking in the lounge and one mentioned he used to work for Fisher Yates where I had worked so I entered into the conversation and we were soon well away, talking about old times. He said he remembered me and I hadn't changed, well it was only about fifty-three years ago. That is the third time I have met someone from the past while on holiday. I had two nice days at Clacton, outings arranged by Ivy Lane.

I have enjoyed various activities to do with the church, one whole day helping to serve refreshments to 300 clergy at a Synod held at a neighbouring church which was not heated and everyone was perished. We served tea and coffee at 11 o'clock and again at lunchtime, they brought their own sandwiches and we served a buffet about 5 o'clock.

I think the good ladies who prepared the food thought they were providing for the five thousand, I have never seen so much food on tables the whole length of a large room. It didn't all go and some of the ministers took some because a lot of them had long journeys, and the helpers had some too. One Friday we went to mend some chairs, they have a shelf under the seat where we put our hymn books and they had come unstuck, so got some glue and restuck them but they haven't lasted. On the Monday after our Harvest a few of us packaged the fruit which we distributed to our house-bound members and Sisterhood. Our Wives Club every year at Christmas, cooks, serves and entertains about 120 folk who suffer from Multiple Sclerosis, our minister takes a great interest in this work. The wives who used to entertain us at concerts always wore a dainty little apron and as they were getting a bit tatty Beatie asked me if I would make fourteen new ones, a pleasure.

I am always busy doing jobs like shortening coats and dresses.

This year Kathy and I had two weeks at Worthing and Olive joined us for our second week. On the August Bank Holiday Monday they had a carnival and we had a splendid view from the balcony and Kathy took some snaps. While roaming round the shops we found one that sold transfers, nice ones that you cannot get nowadays so bought a good amount.

On the 15th September happy news of a new Prince to be called Harry, it helps to brighten up the news, and now we hear of the terrible famine in Ethiopia then the bomb on the Grand Hotel at Brighton in the early hours of the morning at the Conservative Conference. Now we are preparing for Christmas, a time I love, have heard several people say they will be glad when it is all over. If one has lost a dear one that is readily understood, otherwise I think it is a happy time, after all it is a birthday.

Some little time ago we had disturbing news of Christopher, Evelyn's son-in-law, he has a form of cancer in the neck. He has had operations and treatment and is very brave and means to fight it, we are all praying for him and his wife Sally and their two little girls, Lucy and Verity Jane only four months old. A few months ago I saw Christopher in 'Songs of Praise' he was in the choir. I have just returned from seeing them all when I went to Evelyn's on Boxing Day, by appearances he looks well has lost a little weight, but is in good spirits. Left there about 9.30 and was given a lift to the hotel where I spend the night and come home after breakfast, a nice finish to the holiday. Had a pleasant surprise for Christmas Day, an invitation from our minister the Revd John Clapham and his wife to have Christmas dinner and later tea at the manse which I thought very kind.

Ending my Story

Now I think it is time to bring this story to a close. I have enjoyed writing it, I only wish I was a better writer, I do admire a good hand. I hope it has not been too boring, I have tried to make it as interesting as possible. I have not had a bad life, had good parents and grandparents and patient teachers, my mother who taught me my prayers and looked after me and my many friends. To those people who get depressed or feel lonely and friendless we all have one friend, which brings me to the words of my favourite hymn,

> 'What a friend we have in Jesus,
> All our sins and griefs to bear.
> What a privilege to carry,
> Everything to God in prayer.

Oh! what peace we often forfeit.
Oh! what needless pain we bear.
All because we do not carry,
Everything to God in prayer.'

Most of us worry at some time and often the things we worry about don't happen, and it is the little things we are led to do that make a big issue in our lives. Like an invitation to a cup of tea that led to my parents' marriage, and that little dose of whisky that gave my mother another fifty years of life.

A Winter Holiday 1985

The first time I went on holiday in the winter was on the 3rd December for two weeks to Bognor, and we were blessed with good mild weather, only had one nasty wet day. We walked along the front every morning and could sit for a while then made our way to the shopping centre and had a coffee. I don't think there were many shops I didn't go into, first browsing around, and purchased several small items that I couldn't get in London.

I also went to the Methodist church bazaars and bought six jigsaws, one morning we had a small coach to take some of us to Chichester.

One evening at the hotel a group of eight young people came and sang carols and told us how fortunate they were to live in such a nice town. Another evening there was a beautifully illuminated chariot coming along the road with several men dressed as Santa Claus and singing carols, one of them came in and he collected money for his church. Altogether it was a very Christmassy atmosphere and on the Sunday morning at the Methodist church all the young people and children brought gifts to lay at the foot of the Christmas tree, these were later sent to the National Children's Home.

It was a very pleasant fortnight and not boring as I took plenty to occupy me, books, embroidery and even Christmas cards to do, coming home with one week to see to my final Christmas preparations.

As usual I went to Thornton Heath on Boxing Day and stayed at the Norfolk overnight, travelling on the buses was more pleasant than on ordinary week-days.

In January I went to the Palladium to see Cinderella with Anna Neagle. That same night I was woken by knocking at 10.50 to be told there was a gas leak, it was turned off at the meter which left me without any means of getting a hot drink but my kind neighbour next door lent me an electric jug and about 5 o'clock the following day the gas company issued us with an electric hot-plate.

5th February brought us our first snow and then good news that our library had reopened after five months when they had been on strike.

Last November I lost one of my oldest friends, Amy, whom I had known since 1940 when she came to work at my firm. We had many happy outings and holidays together, but of late she became very feeble and went to live in Sunshine Lodge, a home for the elderly, where I visited her many times. When I went to her funeral I saw her nephew Irving and family and was informed she had left me £100. Also saw Vernon, another nephew who had worked at the same firm since he left school. I went there in 1934 and he had then been there about two years, I had not seen him since I retired. I shall miss Amy.

April 21st 1986 was our Queen's 60th birthday, how she is loved by the children with arms full of daffodils to present to her, it was a wonderful occasion.

During May I had an attack of arthritis in my foot, every step was agony. I sent for the doctor and he gave me a letter for the hospital but had to wait four months before I saw the doctor. In the meantime it had improved, after all that wait I had a blood test, but I had taken to using a stick which was a great help. I had to cancel several outings but did however go to Clacton for the Sunday School trip with Olive.

23rd July, another lovely day to remember the wedding of Prince Andrew to Sarah Ferguson, now Duke and Duchess of York. She wore a beautiful ivory satin dress, and train over seventeen feet long, eight young attendants all well behaved, one was Prince William. They left for their honeymoon to the Azores from Chelsea Hospital by helicopter. A lovely happy girl and a very nice natural couple, weather was good only two little showers, I stayed in all day watching television.

One evening in July our minister arranged for a coach to take us to see the Thames Barrier at Woolwich and then on to Caterham to a boys' school that first opened to educate ministers' sons. The headmaster and his wife made us very welcome and we sat down to coffee and cakes, left about ten and got to bed at 12.15.

We now have a new hospital all very nice and modern with unisex wards, what would our ancestors say? In August I had a week at Bognor and in September we had our usual holiday at Worthing, me, Margery, Kathy and Olive. One of the highlights was seeing the carnival from our balcony. What a day, it simply poured but they carried on, we felt so sorry for them. We went to a Handicraft Fair and one afternoon went to Brighton, I wanted to see the Grand Hotel and how they had rebuilt part of it after the bombing. You could not see any difference between old and new.

We usually view any new flats that are going, one was £55,000 but we preferred one that was £44,000, no harm in dreaming. The evening we returned home Kathy and I went to the Wives 25th Anniversary at Dalston Church a very enjoyable evening. The Young Wives Club came about twenty-five years ago with two ladies having a chat over a cup of tea, one a Deaconess at Hackney Central Hall, the other Mrs Rose Cook, were discussing various meetings and that is how the YW Club was born. Over the years many members had become grand-mothers so it was renamed 'The Wives Club'. They meet every Thursday evening and do various things in handicrafts, sort jumble, decorate the church for Christmas and Harvest, raise money for charities and have outings.

During the year we have several coffee mornings, at our last one we raised £91 and then our bazaar when I took £70 on my apron stall. Sometimes I go to Olive's church, 'The Lighthouse' in Markhouse Road for a coffee morning.

In December I had a phone call from the niece of my old

boss, Mrs George as we called her, to say she had died aged ninety-two. Went to Bognor again just before Christmas, same period as last year, for two weeks, could have stayed for another two weeks but had had enough. There is a house at the end of the road called 'Ashley House' that is for sufferers of Multiple Sclerosis, they had their Christmas bazaar and had a table loaded with jigsaws so I went to town as they say and bought eight, a good job my good neighbour Ernie met me on my return home in his car. I came home with a very sore throat and knew I was in for a cold, which I had and a cough, all over Christmas and did not feel at all well. I was quite content to be on my own over the holiday but again my good neighbours asked me to spend Christmas Day with them and their daughter Joyce, they made me very welcome and I enjoyed it as much as you can when you don't feel well.

I paid my usual visit to the chiropodist, I take a little present for each of the two young women who are both very nice and they offered me a sherry, mince pie and a Christmas cracker.

Norman and Susan came the Sunday before Christmas, I have not seen any of them for a year, we exchanged presents.

I was not feeling well on Boxing morning, there was a ring at the door and there stood a nurse who said she was a midwife. I had to convince her I didn't need one.

It is not often one gets a real bargain. I sometimes go to Well Street market and see Beaty where we get material, I get some for my aprons. One Saturday morning the stall holder wanted to dispose of three black bags of small pieces for £1. Beaty and her son Peter took them home and I helped sort them out, just the thing that appeals to me. Anyway to make a long story short, for my £1 have made forty-eight aprons, relined a coat, made two blouses and gave two bags of pieces to two friends.

On the 25th November had a very nice day out by coach from the Salvation Army Centre in Clapton with my neighbours, Lou and Ernie May, who go there. We stopped at

Toddington for a very nice lunch, oxtail soup, fish, chips and peas, followed by trifle and a cup of tea, then we made our way to Milton Keynes in Buckinghamshire. We went on the M25, a 1¹/₂ hours ride then to the shopping centre all under cover. It is vast and beautifully decorated for Christmas for the children. In the middle of January 1987 we had a very cold week with lots of snow, so as usual I stayed put and didn't go out, afraid of slipping, but I was well stocked with food. At the end of the week I was getting a little short, when I had a visit from two angels of mercy, one a lady from the church, Beaty, who rang me and asked me if I needed anything, the other my neighbour's son, so I was very fortunate and count my blessings. The snow cleared for me to see 'Jack and the Beanstalk', another Salvation Army outing at Wimbledon.

January 1987

Now I have finished this catalogue of events and wonder what is on the agenda for the future. Those of us who live in these flats know we are going to see great changes, improvements mainly for the future generation, most of us are contented with things as they are with perhaps a few adjustments, but the powers that be are making great alterations which will require all of us to move. We have had private visits from architects asking us our views and what we wanted and about fifty of us were taken by coach one Sunday morning to view Lea View House, Stamford Hill, to give us an idea of what our flats will be like. (Sunday 2nd November 1986)

We have now got to March, the worst of the weather behind us, not too bad a winter. News of a terrible disaster, Townsend Thoresen ferry, 188 dead.

Walking along Graham Road one morning a young woman stopped me and showing me a coin in the palm of her hand asked, 'Is it any good?' 'It is a pound coin,' I said. She replied she didn't want it and gave it to me.

Another pleasant event was when pensioners were allocated free butter and cheese to dispose of the butter mountain.

In April I lost a very nice friend, Gladys, and two other nice ladies, Elsie and Evelyn's mother.

On the 3rd June I saw the Trooping the Colour on television, it was unusual to see our Queen not riding Burmese but in Queen Victoria's ivory coach. The 11th June we had a general election when Mrs Thatcher was returned, when they were talking about elections on the news apparently we had two general elections in one year 1974. We also saw pictures of the Duke and Duchess of York on the Canadian tour, how happy and natural they both were, if a little dignity has vanished happy informality has taken over.

In June we seemed to have everlasting rain, the wettest June so far, so we were fortunate when we had our annual outing to Clacton in having a very nice day. I went on another outing from the Round Chapel to Broadstairs, a very warm and sunny day, but not without incident. On the way we had a burst tyre and had to wait $1^1/2$ hours for them to send for a mechanic who took about half an hour to change the wheel while we all sat in the coach. Our first port of call was the restaurant where we had a lovely lunch, a lady coming out suddenly collapsed and was taken by ambulance to hospital and stayed in for a few days.

Our minister arranged a day out for us to Whipsnade Zoo, but there was too much walking and not much to see. I had an unexpected invitation from a friend of Helen's to go to a concert at the Hackney Empire and to hear John Evans the Welsh tenor, it was in aid of the children of Hackney, but a bit eerie walking home at 11.15.

It is strange what one remembers and what one doesn't, things that happened in my childhood are very clear to me and more recent things are not. Speaking to an insurance agent a while back the question arose as to what date my mother died, when I told him he looked amazed, 'How do you remember so precisely the date?' he said. I replied, 'There are some dates one never forgets.' I expect he would have been more surprised if I had told him the dates of my father's and both grand-parents' deaths.

At the end of August our much longed for holiday came as usual to Worthing, Kathy, Margery and myself, to be joined by Olive on our second week but we were all disappointed when owing to bad influenza she had to stay home in bed. We had fairly good weather, there was a full moon, lovely to lie in bed and see it shining on the rippling water. We saw the carnival on the Monday and visited a Crafts Fair.

We do tend to buy things when on holiday, one reason I think because there is more time to look around. We could not have these holidays if we didn't have a car to bring us home, my neighbour Mr May, I am afraid he had a shock when he saw us with all our bits and pieces. I also was not well when I went and had to go to the local doctor and was given some anti-biotics so enjoyed my second week. Feeling a bit sorry for myself I saw a girl in a wheelchair minus one leg and both arms, that certainly made me count my blessings. Also going to church on the Sunday morning we saw an old lady with her husband in a wheelchair she said she couldn't see properly and was giddy so we helped her heave the chair up the slope.

This year we seem to have had more than our share of disasters, first the Zeebrugge ferry, 188 dead, the Hungerford mass murder when a man went berserk killing 16 people and injured 23 others.

On the night of 16th October we had a hurricane, gales 110 miles an hour the worst in living memory, all London blacked out for the first time since the war, everywhere you walked the following day there were trees uprooted and no end of damage. Seven Oaks has now lost six of its beautiful trees and Kew Gardens lost thousands of its valuable trees and will never be the same again, but worst of all was the loss of life and great damage to property and cars and many homes without electricity for days and some weeks. Some days after we had torrential rain flooding many places, on the night of the gale most people got up and some made tea but amidst it all I woke up for a few minutes then went off to sleep again, when I sleep I sleep.

On Armistice Sunday at Enniskillen a bomb exploded as people stood round their war memorial.

In the evening of 18th November there was a fire on an escalator at King's Cross, 31 killed and many burned and injured. It is wonderful to see so much bravery of people giving their lives to save others and the generosity of the public to the appeals made to give a little help to those in need.

Now Christmas is upon us, a holiday I always enjoy. It seemed extra long this year as Christmas Day was on a Friday and a good many firms closed for the following week. The weather was exceptionally mild 50–55 degrees, this did not please folks who went to Switzerland for skiing as there wasn't any snow. Now we have the new year to look forward to and may it bring peace.

January 1988

Now another new year has started and during the year nothing very eventful has happened as far as I am concerned only that I have had some nice days out and three very enjoyable holidays. In April Olive and I had a day out, 'Daffodil Sunday', a coach took us to Triplow, a village fete was in progress with all the ancient crafts and Morris dancing and on the way there we stopped at Cambridge for lunch. Another day we went to Finchingfield, also a pretty little village in Essex and had a ploughmans lunch at the Fox Inn.

On the 4th June Kathy and I went to Eastbourne for a week, we stayed at 'West Rocks' not far from the Wish Tower where there is a little train that takes you to the top. You can sit and have tea and then return by train. One day we went to see

Mildred and Bill at Seaford who were once church members. On June 13th we had our usual Sisterhood outing to Clacton, on the 14th went with Ivy Mitchell to Canterbury. This was put on by the Salvation Army but owing to an hour's delay in starting they decided to go to Broadstairs. On June 23rd I went with the Round Chapel ladies and Ivy M to Worthing so June was a very full month. Kathy and Margery also came with me to Thornton Heath but found it a trying journey as it was a very hot day, we didn't see Susan's new baby, Victoria Rose, born on the 5th June.

Back to Scotland July 1988

Monday 11th. It is eleven years since I went to Scotland and that was with Amy in 1974 and 1977, this time I went with Ivy Mitchell, the first time we have been away together but I am sure we got on alright. Have now got to the stage (owing to arthritis) when I hope I don't spoil my companion's holiday because I cannot do a lot of walking or do many steps and stairs, but always say to them you go where you like. We started off before 7 a.m. for the coach station near Upper Woburn Place, Wallace Arnold Tours, had a comfortable sit down watching all the other travellers, then it was our turn to go to South Mimms joining point just off the M25, for 12 days to Strathpeffer. After alighting for coffee, lunch and tea we arrived at the Royal Station Hotel, Newcastle for one night's stay. They had two most beautiful chandeliers.

Tuesday, off again to make our way to Fort William, all round Loch Ness (we didn't see the monster) and Glen Coe where the Campbells killed the Macdonalds, cold icy weather, all dark mountains and very weird. Then on to Gretna Green where we stopped for lunch, we had two nice fine days. Then to Crait Anna Hotel (have been before) very modern but no lift.

Wednesday, left about 9 for our main stay of seven nights at the Ben Wyvis Hotel, Strathpeffer, a very large house in the centre of a small park where the grounds were kept beautifully, flowers and fir trees, the ground not flat but rising and falling. The house was built in 1877 for the factor of Cromarty Estates. We each had a front bedroom and the view was lovely, the ground rising up with rows of different houses and trees and mountains in the background. We visited a small soap factory and saw toilet soap made where Gloria Hunniford's sister works. There was entertainment most evenings, Scottish dancing, a troupe of young girls all ages, the youngest about three. One day of rest we walked round the little village and into some shops which took less than half an hour, into a dolls' museum then coffee in the bakers shop which proved very handy for tea and snacks. In the evening we were taken by coach to Inverness to see some more Scottish dancing, singing and music, all very nice.

Friday, off to Ullapool fishing port, fish and chips for lunch. We arrived back at the hotel just in time to see the bride and guests as there was a wedding on and managed to take a snap of her from my bedroom window. As the wedding party were using the hotel we had our dinner in a marquee which was very nice, we lined up with our plate with meats, salad and fresh salmon and later for our sweet then went back to the hotel for our coffee, it made quite a change.

Saturday, went to the Black Isle and saw the oil rigs, went to a sleepy little village with nobody about, shops not open yet, had coffee at an Inn and walking along Ivy noticed in the corner of a doorway high up three little heads of baby house-martins. We had buffet lunch in the hotel, during our days out went into numerous mills and woollen shops, see one and you see them all.

Sunday, no chance to go to a kirk, driving all day, salmon lunch at Drumchork Lodge, Ross-shire, visited some gardens and craft shop, wet day, had tea and biscuits at Ledgowan Hotel.

Monday, over the ferry to Skye. Not a bad day saw a rainbow.

Tuesday, shops in the morning at Dingwall, a nice little town and shopping area, went over Dewar's whisky distillery and had lunch. The station at Strathpeffer is not used but has been converted into a lovely garden and picnic area with small shops on the platform and a 'Cinema' open three times a day for half an hour to show a film of the Highlands for a pound, we went and there were only seven of us.

Wednesday, left our hotel after seven nights and went on to Perth to the Salutation Hotel (have been before), the oldest hotel in Scotland, no lifts but lovely dining room where you had your starters then walked up to the carvery, took a plate on a wooden platter where the chef carved any meat you liked, I had turkey then helped myself to vegetables. We had stopped for lunch at Luggies and for a sweet had the biggest raspberries I have ever seen with cream.

Thursday, left at 9 for our last night at Stockport, the Belgrade Hotel, all very smart but poor service. At breakfast after a while we were given bacon and egg, we were not asked, fourteen pieces of toast between the two of us and no tea till we asked for it and then only one cup. After dinner there was an antiques fair on. We had lunch at Gretna Green again.

Friday, we left Stockport and the end of our twelve days tour, had coffee near Birmingham, lunch at Northampton and went over a shoe warehouse, then on to South Mimms where we waited with our trolley of luggage for the coach to take us to our starting off point, Upper Woburn Place, where we were lucky in getting a taxi and I was indoors by six o'clock. All in all a very nice holiday but a bit tiring. The splendid scenery and changing sky would be very interesting to an artist, also the waterfalls. It stays lighter about one hour in Scotland and the water is as soft as velvet. We had done over 2,000 miles. One thing I forgot to mention was the trees, so many of them diseased, what leaves there were were grey and withered, we wondered if it was due to acid rain. Talking of trees, on a day's outing to Eastbourne we saw the devastation caused by the hurricane last October for mile after mile trees were bent and broken, it was a very sad sight and will take years of work to put it straight.

One can always find something humorous in one's travels and it seems when you go to Scotland you need long arms. In the dining room at our first hotel they had about six very large round tables which seated about eight people, it was quite amusing at breakfast time when we were trying to reach the condiments and couldn't until someone stood up and passed them round.

We had bath, toilet and all facilities in each hotel but there again a long arm would have been useful, the toilet roll was placed about a yard away from the loo, just the sort of thing Esther Rantzen would include in her programme.

September, our annual visit to Worthing, Margery, Kathy and Olive joined us for our second week. We arrived in time for coffee and were taken by our good friend Ernie May. We didn't do anything very exciting, went to the Crafts Fair and Kathy bought a lovely picture, I bought some home made chocolate. One evening we went to see Russ Conway, and had two enjoyable afternoons seeing a film, 'Little Dorrit'. As usual we saw the carnival from our balcony window on holiday Monday, they were blessed with a fine day. We arrived home in time for our harvest festival.

Late September Kathy, Margery and myself went with other friends from the Round Chapel to Southend and Westcliff, a very nice day. It was time now to prepare for our coffee mornings and bazaar, took £52. Olive and her friend Hilda helped me on my stall I had such a lot of stuff.

In November I was unable to go out owing to arthritis in my

Edith Scott aged 77, taken at breakfast at Paignton in May 1989.

foot and had to ask friends and neighbours to do some necessary shopping. As much as one likes to be independent there comes a time when you need help. I applied for a home help but she didn't arrive till after Christmas by which time I am glad to say my foot was better, still painful when walking but managed to get out. Had two nice afternoons with the Salvation Army, one was a friendly meeting and carols followed by tea and cakes, next day a ride to Basildon shopping centre, a nice outing with Lou and Ernie and Florrie Gough.

The Sunday before Christmas Evelyn and Norman came for an hour and we exchanged presents. I spent Christmas day with the May family.

So ends another year with several sad disasters, the Armenian earthquake 25,000 dead. Then the train crash at Clapham Junction, followed by a Pan Am plane that fell on the village of Lockerbie, 259 dead. It always seems worse just before Christmas. Summing up it has been one of the mildest winters so far in Europe and I think a year of more hope where peace is concerned.

1989

We shall not see our minister for three months, he is going on a sabbatical

A strangeness for me is that instead of launching into 1989 with you and the unfolding of a new year with its new possibilities of the Kingdom, I shall be away. Perhaps most of you know I shall be on a 'sabbatical' from January to March.

Last year Methodism introduced for its ministers a sabbatical system: once every seven years a minister is given 3 months in which to take up some kind of project, free of any Circuit responsibilities. It may be travel or study or working down a coalmine (or in a beauty-parlour!). My 'turn' has come up in this current Methodist year 88/89. I was going to go to the West Indies to do some study, but my Mother has now gone permanently into hospital after a crisis which means that she is only just holding onto some kind of recognition of me as 'family'. So I can't go far away. In fact, I shall be just north of London and will be attempting some writing to do with India and with faith. Meg will join me at the weekends and the Manse is being kept an eye on.

Rev John Clapham BA

We don't seem to have started the new year very well, with yet another disaster, a plane came down on the M1 motorway killing 44 people.

On the 10th January Lou and I went to see Aladdin at the Hackney Empire. At last on the 9th Hilda moved to the flat next to Ellen's, several of us helped, Beaty did most because she is tough, and her two sons Nigel and Peter laid all the carpet. I shortened the curtains and helped unpack numerous boxes with Kathy and Rose. She will be much happier there.

They do say things get earlier every year, we get Christmas cards in the shops in August but hot cross buns in M&S on 6th January is a bit much.

At the end of January our minister lost his mother, she was 90 and had been ill some time. John took several of us in a mini bus to Brookside Methodist Church, East Barnet, for the service then to St Pancras cemetery for the cremation and back to Brookside for a lovely repast. In her younger days she (Dora) had been a deaconess and started life in Bow with her husband also a minister and when he retired they went to live at East Barnet, she was a much loved and lovely lady.

During March I had not been feeling well for some weeks, everything was an effort, I had to sit down once or twice when washing up. On the Wednesday I attempted to go to Sainsbury's as usual and knew I couldn't make it so came back and rang my doctor, he came the following morning and said when I was a little better he would like me to go to hospital for a check-up and gave me a prescription. Knowing I couldn't get out I rang my good neighbours and Joyce handed it in at the chemists and called for it on her way home from work. I became very thirsty and asked the milkman if he had any fruit drinks so he went to his float to get some pineapple juice and when he returned I was on the floor unconscious. I had no warning and don't know anything about it, what a shock he had. Luckily the doctor next door was taking his surgery and they laid me on my bed and he rang for an ambulance. When I came to a strange lady was looking at me, I asked what happened. She said, 'You collapsed, they have rung for an ambulance.' This was about 11 o'clock. I had several tests and X-rays, one on my head where I knocked it and at about four o'clock was told I had anemia so had two blood transfusions.

My chief worry was that Joyce would be ringing my bell and no one to answer it, I had most phone numbers in my bag but not theirs, so asked a nurse for the directory for M. She came back and said they only had one from A to K. Eventually when Joyce got no reply she and her father looked through my windows, saw I was not there and the bed not made and concluded I must be in hospital. She rang Homerton and heard I was there. Next day I had more tests and had a gastroscopy, a tube with a light on the end put down your throat to examine the stomach as they thought I had a bleeding ulcer, without exaggeration it was torture. I learned later it is customary to give some form of anaesthetic, they must have thought I was tough.

What most people need when ill is rest. Saturday nights they are extra busy with accident cases, broken limbs mostly, a nice young woman next to me had a broken leg. She and her husband had gone to the Lea Valley ice rink to celebrate their wedding anniversary and she slipped and fell, they lived at Epping but Homerton was the nearest hospital. We didn't have our nightly drink till after 11 o'clock. When you eventually dropped off you were awakened about two to take a pill and blood pressure taken. I happened to be there on Mothering Sunday. The hospital chaplain, a fine American gentleman enquired if I would like to attend the service but I didn't feel well enough so he gave me some daffodils. It was a beautiful sunny day, 5th March and many visitors, children and grandchildren came to see mum or grandma, one couple brought their four children, so nicely dressed and very well behaved, a tonic these days, one little boy brought over a box of chocolates and asked me to take one.

I was in there just a week, quite an experience and it makes you count your blessings. When I was thinking of coming home, what to do about clothes? I only had my nightie and dressing gown and slippers, when I first went in I didn't have anything, soap, flannel or toothbrush, gradually my kind friends brought these things in. Kathy, Margery and Olive were all very kind and I asked Margery if she would go to my home and get me some clothes. I had two offers to bring me home, Beaty and Alf collected me and we did some shopping on the way home as the cupboard was bare.

I had eleven visitors, Margery several times, Kathy, Olive, Rose Cook, Ernie May, Kenneth Glendinning, one of our ministers, Eddie and Ivy Lane, Ivy Mitchell and Helen Fribbance and eleven get well cards. How lovely when lying in bed to see a friendly face coming towards you and how fortunate to have so many kind friends. It appears I didn't have an ulcer but inflammation of the stomach and shall have to take iron tablets for a good while. I felt very weak for some time, but thanks to Dial-a-ride could do my own shopping. (Well I never! looking back I had five men in my bedroom in one morning.)

Odd bits of News

On the 26th April I went with Lou May from the Congress Hall, to the Royal Albert Hall for the celebration of the Salvation Army's 'Pearl Anniversary' of the over 60s Club. We heard Moira Anderson and Robert Dougal give a talk, a very nice afternoon.

In Mare Street, what is known as the Narrow Way is being repaired as the road was sinking and will be completed about October, it is being made into a shopping precinct. Also we now have a smart shopping centre all under cover but alas no seats or toilet, it is called Dalston Cross, a few yards from Ridley Road.

In one of the letters in the *TV Times* there was a request for people to write in about all the old films and stars and old cinemas, I enjoyed writing a long letter, and received a nice reply.

One can often see something interesting when in the street or perhaps waiting for a bus. One morning I saw a young man with two panes of glass (wrapped up) and two heavy bags of shopping waiting to get on a bus. A young woman helped him with his bags, but of course you cannot use public transport if you are carrying glass, I wondered what the poor chap would do and how he would get home.

At the same bus stop a man came along with bags of shopping and one toppled over spilling the contents, grape-fruits, onions etc. into the road. Well Dalston Junction is a very busy thoroughfare and along came a juggernaut but the driver was good enough to stop and folks helped the man gather his stuff.

I have just been looking at one of my favourite programmes, 'Heirloom' with John Bly, similar to the Antiques Road Show. He had a guest expert, Henry Sandon, a very pleasant and jovial character talking about candle extinguishers or snuffers, it appears they were used because it was considered indelicate for a lady to blow them out, some were as much as £4,000.

I wrote a letter to the *Hackney Gazette* about not having any seating in our new Dalston Cross and they printed it, but still no seats.

Some years ago I had to find a new hairdressers as where I used to go they had retired. On the way to my shopping I noticed a place called 'The Smart Set'. I felt a bit hesitant about going in, thought it might be one of those ultra modern places, on the contrary it is a very homely place and Malcolm who owns it is always nice and obliging also Pat. The clientele are mostly pensioners, a good many are neighbours where I live.

Holidays

On the 6th May we went to Congress Hall with Mays for a holiday at Paignton, arranged by the Salvation Army. Our first stop was Swindon for a 45 minute lunch break, then after another short break we arrived at 3.40. We toured so many places, Brixham, Torquay, Dartmoor and Widdicombe where we had tea in the gardens served by young women dressed like Lorna Doone. In the evening we went to a show to see Ruby Murray and her son and John Boulter. The Princess Theatre on the front was taken over by the Salvation Army for the week, there was something on nearly every evening. We had a whole day out to Exeter, a lovely busy town and shopping centre with plenty of small buses of different colours, I was very lucky to get some transfers which I cannot get in London, then on to Dawlish. The following day we went to Cockington where I enjoyed a ride in a pony and trap. We rode through Babbacombe and in the evening attended a male voice choir. Thursday out all day to Dartmouth and Selbourne, coming home we had to wait an hour to cross the ferry. We saw the illuminations at Torquay Friday and our last day I spent on my own, all around the shops and in the evening to the Salvation Army for party night and refreshments.

Saturday we left at 9 o'clock, had two short stops and arrived at Clapton at 3.30, a nice young Salvationist brought us home in his car. Altogether a very enjoyable holiday it was all go, good weather and good food and very reasonable.

10th June Kathy, Olive and I went to Eastbourne, lovely weather went on the little train to Holywell had tea and walked back. We had a coach ride to Bramber village and went in the House of Pipes, every conceivable shape of pipe (smoking) tobacco tins, old cigarette packets and match boxes. This was our second visit to Eastbourne in recent years, we feel more at home at West Rocks. A group of nice ladies go every year so they can all meet, one very elderly lady is terribly crippled with arthritis one leg bent nearly in half. The staff are very kind to her and take her to the dining room in a wheel chair. She can never go out, but one day a young man who was staying only one night at the hotel very kindly took her in the chair along the sea front, it was a lovely change for Elsie, but a terrible job to get the chair up and down the steps with her in it. He came and chatted with the ladies and made us all laugh, he had rung his wife and said he had been along the front with another woman and his wife would be seeing a solicitor tomorrow. What a nice man to give an old lady such a treat, it made our day.

26th August, Worthing, again four of us, Margery joined us, she needed a holiday after being mugged by two girls when visiting a neighbour in Homerton Hospital, and Olive too needed a change, her mother was very ill and her job was unsteady. Kathy too had not been well, so we all went in a car from door to door what a treat, but we all felt tired and I felt very sleepy, had lovely weather. We didn't do much, had a ride to High Salvington and saw the windmill and one evening saw Edmund Hockridge, a nice family show with his wife and two sons, he is seventy and a Canadian.

Days Out

20th June, a mystery tour which turned out to be Suffolk, Constable Country, Bury St Edmunds and Dedham one of the hottest days of the year. Ivy M and I were pleased to find a shady seat in some lovely gardens.

3rd July went to Hastings and spent the day with Gladys D, the first time we have been out. Went up in the lift and sat watching the lovely view eating our sandwiches, on our way there in the coach we saw one of our old ministers the Revd Healey. Went round a market and then on to Hythe and had a nice tea and coming home Ernie met Lou, Florrie and me and brought us home in his car.

July 21st Said farewell to Asha and Revd Kenneth Glendinning at Chatsworth, they are going to Scotland.

8th August A day touring Norfolk, Hunstanton and Kings Lynne with Gladys again, went to see some lavender fields.

10th October A day in Kent, coffee at Tunbridge Wells, lunch in Folkestone and tea in Herne Bay with Ivy M.

All these outings were arranged by the Salvation Army at Cambridge Heath and Congress Hall at Clapton and they were all enjoyable. True we have had a lovely summer, the hottest since 1976, 91 degrees sometimes and of course a shortage of water in many parts.

While at Eastbourne we saw Harry Secombe, he had been recording at the bandstand for Highway and waved to us as he walked along, what a lovely person he is. I get a lot of pleasure from my television. On 'Woman of the Year Awards' at the Savoy Hotel, someone told the story of a professor from Yale University who got up to speak at a dinner. He said every letter stands for a good meaning for young people, so he spent fifteen minutes on Y which stands for youth, twenty minutes on A for ambition, another fifteen minutes to say L stood for learning and lastly fifteen minutes on E for education. When he had finally ended the chairman got up and thanked him and said they were so pleased he did not come from Massachusetts. We had our bazaar at Dalston Church and handed in £60. I am kept busy one way and another going to Olive's coffee morning, seeing friends in hospital, one was Hilda who had a stroke, pleased to say she is home now and much better.

I missed a nice outing to Reading when I was getting over the flu, in spite of having an injection I felt really ill for several weeks, we have had an epidemic. It amuses Olive when I say I can be ill in comfort simply because when you haven't got to go to work and you have no money worries, not like years ago when you went to work when you were only fit for bed.

I was well enough to see the pantomime 'Babes in the Wood',

and the week after Margery joined me with Lou and Ernie May for a coach ride to Leo's at Chingford for some Christmas shopping. We had a mince pie and a cup of tea then on to Oxford and Regent Street to see the illuminations. It was a pouring wet night and a little thunder and lightning but we were all cosy in the coach. Next morning I went to see Selfridges' windows, always worth seeing, they were ballet scenes, and it took me two hours to get home from just outside the store.

Spent Christmas day with Mays, they hired a hall as it was their Golden Wedding Anniversary.

1990

The time is drawing nearer when I shall be moving. The latest date is end of April but who knows, anyway we went to view a show flat and it all seems very nice. One of the tenants (a Jewish lady) who will be on my floor, happened to meet me one day and in a friendly way she said, 'You look nice, where are you going?' I replied, 'To the Sisterhood, you know the Methodist Church opposite the Town Hall,' 'Oh!' she said, 'aren't you Jewish?' I said no in surprise. She said, 'I thought you were a typical yiddisher woman.'

Strange as it may seem, years ago sitting in Springfield Park talking to a Jewish lady she would not believe I wasn't Jewish. When I told a friend she said, 'Oh yes it's your nose.' I had a good look in the mirror, there certainly is a little bump on the bridge but none of my friends agree.

I had a pleasant surprise with a visit of my two girl cousins, Muriel and Mavis, (3rd cousins actually) hadn't seen them for about three years so you can guess we had plenty to talk about, especially of our families and as I am older than them am able to enlighten them as to what happened years ago. Muriel made a tribute to my father when she said he wasn't only a gentleman but a gentle man.

I had a happy birthday when Kathy, Margery and Olive came for coffee and Helen in the afternoon. I am very fortunate in the friends I have, not many perhaps by other people's standards but those I have are pure gold. I was disappointed on Sunday when Evelyn and Norman didn't come because there was a risk of a severe gale.

We thought October 1987 gales were bad, now on the 25th January we had equally dangerous gales if not worse, 110 miles an hour in some parts, and as the worst part was in the afternoon people could not get home from work, some were lucky enough to spend the night in trains, others just laid on the platforms, at least forty-seven killed in this country alone, and what was shown on the television with people literally thrown off their feet.

In March we had a poll-tax riot, the following morning I walked through the Narrow Way, glass everywhere, hardly a shop front remained intact, from past the Town Hall to Gateways, so many shop fitting vans you could hardly walk along. It was not done just for looting, the hooligans smashed every window, butchers, estate agents and all, just done for devilment.

One good thing, the ambulance strike is over after nearly five months.

Tuesday 17th April went to Folkestone with Ivy Mitchell, had coffee at Tenterdon.

Tuesday 22nd May. Ivy and I went to Worthing which gave me a chance to call at our hotel to arrange for our holidays, we then went on to Brighton.

9th June Kathy and I had a nice week at Eastbourne, where we met the usual group of ladies, we feel more at home there now.

Tuesday 19th June Had a lovely day at the Cotswolds with Lou, it is a beautiful place with pretty villages and little bridges and interesting shops. We went on to Swindon to the large

Davis House Salvation Army building where they have small flats for people to stay who are in various sorts of trouble for temporary accommodation.

Thursday 5th July Gladys and I went to Weymouth with the ladies from the Round Chapel.

Tuesday 17th July off to Hunstanton with Lou and Ernie.

Tuesday 24th July a Mystery Tour with Ivy M. We stopped at Rochester which is a very nice town with nice shops, then on to Cliftonville for lunch where we found a very pleasant newly opened restaurant for fish and chips. We were each presented with a plastic rose.

Tuesday 4th September Went to Tunbridge Wells with Lou, Ernie and Florrie, walked along the Pantiles which derives its name from the square clay tile paving of the walks in 1699, my second visit there.

September 8th We only had a week at Worthing as they had changed hands and we weren't sure what it would be like. Margery, Kathy, Olive and myself enjoyed ourselves and had good weather. I have indeed been fortunate with the weather, have had eight days out and every day perfect.

The Sunday after our holiday I went to church as usual and coming home was to receive a shock. I had just got to my door and having another bag as well as my handbag put them down while I put the key in the lock. A young girl who had followed me in and went up the stairs ran down and snatched my handbag. I called after her to let me have my glasses but of course she didn't stop for that, rang 999 and two policemen came and took all particulars but of course heard nothing more. I did have a look round some of the roads nearby thinking at least the bag might be there but no luck, friends said in a way it was a good job I was not holding the bag because she would have wrenched it off my arm. She must have been very disappointed as only had about £1.50p in it, but it is all the odds and ends one misses when you lose your bag and also my glasses. This is the second time this has happened and each time on a Sunday.

On the same day in the afternoon I went to view my new flat.

Moving Day

Wednesday 26th September At last moving day had arrived, after twenty-four years living here. I had started packing in May as was told I should be moving in June and so it went on, one delay after another. At 8.15 the removal people I wanted (Fisher's) arrived, five men, all finished at ten o'clock. It was an easy move for them from ground floor then about 100 yards to the lift and up to third floor.

There I was with numerous boxes in the centre of the living room but I always think if the floors are done and curtains up it is pretty plain sailing. Kathy had previously come with me to choose the carpets, we were in the shop about an hour, such a variety, also she came with me to buy three armchairs as I had to dispose of my three piece suite. Margery had given me two pairs of curtains to hang up pro tem and Olive helped. I had a good lot of help from Eddie our porter and Bidge, a good friend of Margery's, in hanging curtains putting up pictures and plates and numerous odds and ends as I am handicapped with arthritis and cannot even stand on a chair or lift my arms up very high. Once again God was good to me in receiving all this help.

I have had no end of workmen to see to heating and hot water, also carpenters as after the carpet was laid all the doors had to come off, what a mess.

Although a bit tired I had enjoyed it all in putting things in new places, some of the things had been packed so long had forgotten I had them.

Now one expects teething troubles in a new building, we did not have hot water for seven weeks, no baths and kettles on for everything, thank goodness we had a launderette. Another problem was the heating, when turned on full was stone cold so more engineers and architects who said the valves were faulty so fit new ones. After a few days when the weather had turned humid we turned them down and sometimes completely off but they were boiling so I opened all the windows as I cannot stand a lot of heat. Now after 17 weeks they are working properly.

I have had a good many visitors and everyone seems to like it and said it is more like an hotel.

As you enter the foyer there is a very large lounge comfortably furnished in easy chairs in several pastel shades and chintz curtains and lampshades and from there leads to a small conservatory. The landscape back and front was supposed to have cost £5,000. The flat has gas central heating, otherwise all electric which I have got used to but prefer gas for cooking. There are two blocks of 37 flats, one and two bedrooms, including one with facilities for a wheelchair and we have a warden.

I had seventeen 'New Home' cards, and also many visitors. We have had two Christmas parties, also on Wednesday 17th October we had a trip to Southend to see the illuminations. We started off about 4.45 and of course came into all the heavy traffic, it was stop and start for miles. We arrived at 8 o'clock and most of us were starving, not having anything since luncheon and thinking we were stopping for tea. We found a nice fish shop and enjoyed a good meal, arrived home 11.45.

A Day to Remember

A day we had been looking forward to for some time, Friday 30th November, we were going to entertain royalty. We had already received an invitation to meet the Duke of Gloucester who was coming to open our flats officially, he was due at 11 o'clock, so I went down to the lounge at ten. There was such a gathering, about 130 present I would think including our directors and the staff (because they own a considerable amount

107

of property). It being a Jewish concern the gentlemen wore their capels.

We had Jewish caterers and wine and plenty of waitresses. He viewed two flats and asked one lady if he could see her kitchen again. 'Is it always as tidy as this?' he asked? 'Oh! yes Sir,' she replied. 'I am a very tidy person.' Then he unveiled the plaque and chatted to several tenants, he seems a very nice homely man.

The photographers were busy. I was asked if when he was leaving would I thank him for coming but I declined and a Jewish gent did the honours.

I came upstairs at four o'clock having enjoyed a very happy and different sort of day.

Odd items of news

Evelyn and Norman's middle daughter had a son on 6th November, he is named Benedict and the first boy in the family for some time.

November, Mrs Margaret Thatcher has resigned as Prime Minister and we now have John Major who seems a very nice man.

11th December went with Mays on a Christmas shopping trip arranged by the Salvation Army, first to London Colney to Savacentre (Sainsbury's) so huge one didn't know where to start, then on to St Albans with its quaint little shops, then back on the coach home to the Salvation Army's Congress Hall in Clapton to a very nice Christmas dinner and a present, then driven home by Ernie and Lou. Indoors by 4.20, they have now moved and I shall miss them.

I had a very quiet Christmas, had a very bad cough and cold, don't think I have ever coughed so much before so there was no place like home, a number of people have had this virus, it was three weeks before I felt better.

One in our little circle, Margery, was taken ill with a heart attack and was in intensive care and in hospital over Christmas, she is now staying with her good cousins who are kindly looking after her.

It seems to me she has spent most of her life in looking after others, a perfect Christian example.

Also our friend Hilda who was our organist has now gone into a nursing home.

One Sunday morning we had a visiting preacher, the Revd Hurdman from St John's, our parish church. He was very interesting and said how different our church was to his, we are smaller and therefore more cosy and there is a friendly atmosphere, whereas his church is large and the congregation sit rather spaced out and it is cold. I have heard of some folks who even take a hot water bottle with them, who can blame them for being comfortable for an hour or so.

Talking of warmth and comfort I did think living in a centrally heated flat might help my arthritis, but alas it seems worse since I have lived here, I seem to get stiffer and stiffer, it even hurts to dress and undress.

1991

Well we don't seem to have started the new year very well, on Thursday 17th January the Gulf War started and that monster Saddam Hussein has to be conquered, but at what cost. Once again our young men pay the price of freedom and to keep us and others safe, to say nothing of the misery and heartache that is caused to their loved ones, they need our prayers. It ended on the 23rd February.

Never have I seen such heartbreaking pictures as we have seen on our television news of the Kurdish people, no food, no homes trying to get along, leaving their country ankle deep in mud, one old lady on all fours.

Kathy, Rose and I went to see Margery at Loughton where she is staying with those good folks, Barbara and David.

We had a cab when we got off the No 20 bus because it is rather hilly, on our return journey we thought we would walk, someone with a camera should have seen us, Rose taking my arm and helping me up the hill and we just missed a bus by a few seconds. Barbara would have given us a lift there and back had it not been for an accident with her car which was not her fault. It was lovely seeing Margery again after all this time, she is making progress slowly, and seeing Barbara and David in the lovely house. We have been several times and have some lovely snaps of them all, have also got some snaps of the snow we had in February.

Our friend Hilda died on 2nd April after a long time feeling ill and weary, she was a very nice person and we shall miss her. During the summer months I have been to Maldon Park, Bournemouth, Henley-on-Thames, Oxford, Worthing and Bexhill all day trips and Sandown, Eastbourne, and Worthing for holidays.

I feel so fortunate in living where I am, it is all so very nice and always something going on, several things I do not take part in as I have enough to interest me in my flat. We have a mobile library once a month, a keep fit class, bingo, a spelling contest, a free eye test, a talk on crime prevention and fire safety. One evening a fish and chip supper and now and again tea and cakes for someone's birthday, one couple gave a lovely tea for their 53rd Wedding Anniversary. We also have jumble sales. I now have Dial-a-Ride to take me shopping or going a distance and have also taken to using a stick, since living here my arthritis has become a lot worse. We are lucky in having a very nice and helpful warden, Merle.

Beautiful, beautiful said the American lady. it was worth that nine hour flight. There was a re-run on TV of the Prince and Princess of Wales on their 10th wedding anniversary, lovely to see it all again and when you hear the crowds cheering and enjoying it all it makes you proud to be British.

One does not often hear anything on the news to make one laugh but the other day was an exception, a raider in a shop had a surprise before he could get away, when a customer, a hefty 20 stones woman, laid on him till the police arrived.

Fawlty Towers

24th August – 7th September

I was looking forward to our annual holiday at Worthing, we had been to the same hotel for years and had a lovely time but they had changed hands again so we hoped everything would be satisfactory. When we arrived and signed the register the man in charge, of Arab appearance, didn't know the room numbers and another man helping him had only been there a week. I had been handed a menu while sitting in the lounge, there were about eight items for the main course so decided on halibut. On entering the dining room we waited as is customary to be told where to sit. Oh sit anywhere we were told. Looking forward to a lovely meal our hopes were dashed, I asked for tomato soup they hadn't any so I said any soup will do, no halibut only scampi and chips and two other things we didn't fancy, so we asked could they do a salad. When it came just shredded lettuce, a tomato and ham, Kathy's arrived 15 minutes after mine. We were served by the Arab gentleman who hadn't the faintest idea how to wait at table and very slow, someone asked for serviettes and when were they going to be served. We were two hours having our so called dinner, some folks walked out, not stopping for their sweet.

We were both at boiling point and could have walked out, but I simmered down on learning that the staff had all left and realized what a predicament they were in. Breakfast was passable, no porridge, prunes or muesli, only packets of rice crispies and small packets of corn flakes which you had to ask for every morning but I did have a full breakfast every morning and we had a proper waiter but only for breakfast time as he was a student.

It appears the manager didn't come on Saturdays, rather odd as Saturdays are a hotel's busiest day.

We saw him on the Sunday and he was full of apologies and said he would adjust our bills. The manager, a young man complete in denim shorts with fringe and red braces, was not bothered about anything and his favourite reply 'No Problem'. He could not have had any training, his wife cooked Sunday dinner and he got a recipe of his mother's for lamb stew, but as it was a boiling hot day we were not in the mood. They had run out of ice cream so we had trifle which was very nice and some days for dessert they had the most gorgeous black cherries I have ever tasted. On the Tuesday following Bank Holiday Monday he went to cash and carry to stock up and things were better after that. One day we asked could we have peaches and ice cream but they hadn't any.

I am sure I have more food in my cupboard than they have. We never had a cut off the joint the whole fortnight. One day our table was No 4, that's better I thought, another day No 5 and although we had a larger table because there were four of us you would often find other people at your table. I had a word with the manager about keeping one's own table. 'I can put a reserve card on it,' he said, which he did for one meal only. Other holiday makers complained about this, some having to wait for a table, although there was another dining room going spare they didn't seem to have the sense to use it, there was no proper system of doing things in any way. One morning at breakfast Olive asked if we could have our tea now please. 'Yes! I will put the kettle on,' the waiter said.

All this caused a lot of amusement and we had plenty to talk and laugh about. The second week certainly improved but way below standards for what we were paying. I don't think anyone who came our first week would ever come again.

One man when paying his bill said, frankly the service has been a disaster. The lounge was beautifully furnished and the rooms quite nice, but there was only one chambermaid and she didn't have time to hoover any floors.

Margery and Olive who came for our second week were taken by surprise when after signing the register they were asked what they wanted for dinner, there was only one menu which they read out to everyone. In spite of all this trauma we all enjoyed our holiday, perfect weather, good companionship and lots of laughs, as one lady said to stay here you need a good sense of humour.

Once Kathy asked for a glass of orange for starters, the waiter brought one, at the same time the barman brought one. 'Now that's service,' I said. The week after we came home they were going to engage a chef, salary £350 per week.

Amid all the doom and gloom one hears on the television news these days, there were happy news of the release of Terry Waites and all the others who have suffered.

It was amazing how Terry Waites, on his first day of freedom after four years in a dark cell and chained up, no one to speak to only the guard who brought his food, could stand up and speak over fifteen minutes, telling of his experiences of five years as a hostage. He said how once he received a postcard of John Bunyon imprisoned in Bedford jail, he thought he is a lucky chap he has a window, pen and ink to write with and his own clothes. He was in wonderful spirits, only the eyes showed suffering. It is hard to imagine five years and not even seeing the sky.

Our Christmas bazaar raised nearly £368. I handed in £81.55 but a lot of that was work I had done during the year.

We went on a trip to Lakeside, so large you can get lost, which we did by standing at the wrong entrance for our coach, we were nearly half an hour late, you can guess how we felt when we got in the coach.

Then we went on to Southend to see the illuminations but there weren't any, they had been on the night before but not when we went.

Spent a very nice Christmas day with Vera who kindly invited me and made me very welcome. We had a New Year's party here which was very enjoyable.

1992

Early in the New Year I had a visit from two of my third cousins from Greenford, we had plenty to talk about. I gave them a framed water colour of dad's each and one for their brother.

Now I have my birthday to look forward to, I have actually reached 80 but don't feel that age in myself, only in my walking. Evelyn, Norman and Sarah came on Sunday and on Tuesday had tea and cakes downstairs in the lounge.

At the end of March I hope to continue the celebrations on a larger scale.

Celebrations

Friends, neighbours and long lost relatives one could say, it was a gathering for my 80th birthday, actually two months after it because at the end of January we often have bad weather and snow and people wouldn't want to come long distances in that sort of weather, so I postponed it till March 28th, a belated birthday tea from 3–7 o'clock. I could not have held this celebration if I did not live here, I was able to hire our large lounge with kitchen adjoining, very convenient for the caterers all on the level, two toilets and one of the tenants lent me two dress rails for folks to hang their coats on. Extra chairs were brought in as there were about 40 people expected. Two ladies from the Wives Club, Mabel and June, did the catering which was splendid and Mabel's husband Bill helped bring in all the food, tables and tea urn, it was all go. They arrived about 1.30. Kathy was the first to arrive at 2.30 to help as door porter

My cousins, Mavis, Ernie and Hetty, Muriel (sitting).

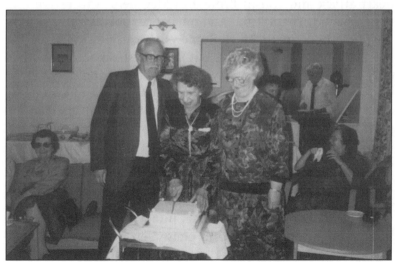

Norman and Evelyn helping me cut the cake.

115

because she was the only one who knew everyone and could let them in if I was not around.

Then they all started arriving, a bit confusing when several all come at once and I could not introduce them to each other as I had intended, but they soon sorted themselves out and got friendly with each other. My cousins Muriel and Mavis who live at Greenford I have seen recently, but their brother Ernie and his wife Hetty I had not seen for 18 years, so it was a proper reunion.

Evelyn and Norman brought the beautiful birthday cake and two sponges which she had kindly made. Their three daughters, two husbands and four children whom I had not seen for years also turned up.

Margery, Barbara and David and Rose came from Loughton.

Our Minister John Clapham and his wife Meg, and our secretary Ivy Lane and husband Eddie and others whom I will mention later. They all had a cup of tea and biscuits on arrival.

Then after a while we had an upset, Eddie collapsed with a heart attack and cousin Ernie and Meg helped to revive him which he did, Thank God. An ambulance took him to our local hospital then on to Bartholomews. He came home on the Monday and is to have tests, but it was a shock to us all, I had only been talking to him a few minutes beforehand.

About 4.30 we had some entertainment, Elsie and Jean doing their mime of 'We're Just a Couple of Swells' all dressed up, then Beaty doing her act of 'Nobody Loves a Fairy over Forty' complete in fairy dress, wand and ballet shoes, all went down very well and little Benedict stood looking in wonderment, Beaty was going to render a couple of monologues but time was running out, our minister acted as compère.

We were now beginning to feel hungry and there was more than enough for everyone and plenty left over, as six of those invited were unable to come.

Then I cut the cake and snaps were taken and I said a few

words, and am pleased to say a good time was had by one and all.

After they had all gone, the wives and Vera and Maureen helped me take things upstairs and finally a wash and bed. I was so tired, too tired even to look at my presents so had a nice morning on Sunday looking at them, it was like Christmas all over again.

Looking back I think I can say it was one of the happiest days of my life, I enjoyed all the arranging and planning.

A few remarked that for my age what a lot of friends I have. Well! I said you gather them through life, what is unusual in my case is with the exception of two of the ladies present they are all younger than me.

It is strange but I had never considered I had many friends but when you start making out a guest list, I got to forty-five and could have gone on and what is best of all they are all loyal. I am pleased to say Eddie fully recovered and seems quite well.

Presents received

Barometer	Bottle Wine
Sandwich Toaster	Toilet bag
Birthday Cake	Vouchers
Flower arrangement	Cash
Wheelbarrow (Royal Doulton)	Handkerchiefs
Hydrangea	Silk scarf
Plant	Snapshots
Twinings Tea-bags	
3 boxes Chocolates	

Those invited

Muriel and Sydney Jackson from Greenford
Mavis Denham from Greenford   } 3rd cousins
Ernie and Hetty Browne from Northolt
Sally and Christopher, Lucy and Verity Jane Reeve from
    Copthorne, Sussex
Susan and Alexis, Victoria and Benedict Stafford from Croydon
Sarah Johnson from Hammersmith
Evelyn and Norman Johnson from Thornton Heath, Surrey
Evelyn and Norman's 3 daughters
Olive Pitterson from Leyton
Kathy Goater from Dalston
Rose Cook from Dalston
Barbara and David Read from Laughton
Margery Stead from Laughton
Rose Gibson from Laughton
Rev John and Meg Clapham from Dalston
Ivy and Eddie Lane from Chingford
Ivy Mitchell from South Hackney
Gladys and Bill Doddimeade from Clapton
Beaty and Alf Final from Hackney
Irene and Marjorie Final from Hackney
Rene Hogarth from Clapton
Vera Noyes from Navareno Mansions
Maureen Morgan from Navareno Mansions
Merle (Warden) and Karen from Navareno Mansions

Wives Club
Mabel, Bill and June
Elsie and Jean
Eileen

The highlights of the summer are our holidays and a few days out, I often wonder how much longer I shall be able to make it, it's not everyone who would want to go away with a person who has difficulty in walking, but I have very patient friends.

Eastbourne in June and Worthing in September, to a new hotel on the other side of the pier near gardens and park, a very pricy place but convenient. Could have had several days out but declined as it is too much of an effort, but we did go to Littlehampton one day, with Kathy, Rose and Gladys. I wasn't sure if I would get to Eastbourne as I had pleurisy in May. Woke up with severe stabbing pains every time I took a breath, but recovered and Kathy said it would be like convalescence.

Nearer the end of the year we had several enjoyable outings, one to Wembley to see Torvill and Dean but having a seat with a long flight of steps to ascend and worse still to come down with nowhere to hold on to was very worrying. Our warden and another lady helped me down.

Then Dial-a-Ride arranged two evening drives, the first a Mystery Tour, started at 6 o'clock, drove all through the East End then all through the West End, saw the *Cutty Sark*, went across the Woolwich Ferry and stopped for refreshments on the Embankment opposite County Hall, had sandwiches, cake and tea or coffee and we didn't have to leave the coach.

Another evening we saw the West End lights which I think were very disappointing, we could only go through part of Oxford Street owing to a bomb going off at 7 o'clock. Stopped again for refreshments in the same place and on the way home drove through Roman Road where the illuminations were beautiful. I noticed how dark some of our London streets are.

Our warden arranged a Christmas dinner at a wine bar, well I expected it to be dimly lit so we groped our way in and it was candlelit, thought of Hyacinth and her candlelight suppers. We could just about see what was on our plates. The food was good, but what really spoilt it there was a noisy party in progress, it was like Bedlam. When the waiter asked what I wanted for a sweet I had to rise from my chair and shout 'Christmas pudding'. We paid £10 and £1 service charge, but we enjoyed it and it was a night out. We also had two Christmas parties here. Spent Christmas and New Year on my own and didn't mind a bit. Took £61 at the bazaar.

Have now got a Home Care person, a nice lady who comes on Friday mornings and goes to Sainsbury's and the Post Office and is a very good shopper. I think of myself although handicapped with arthritis very fortunate, Home Help for shopping, milk delivered, postman, prescriptions and library books brought to my door, window cleaner who puts up clean curtains, launderette and hairdressers downstairs, pillar-box outside the flats, which reminds me of a line from that lovely hymn 'Great is thy Faithfulness, All that I needeth thy hand has provided.'

Living in this lovely place there are six couples and each has a partner who is handicapped in some way, it is good to see how the other partner cares for them. One couple will shortly celebrate their Diamond Wedding.

At our harvest festival it is customary for the children to be at the service, on one occasion we had a lady minister who brought a large map with her so she could show the children where the different foods came from. Picking up a bunch of carrots she enquired, 'Where do these come from?' Up shoots the arm of a little lad who said, 'Tescos'.

Now they say post early for Christmas, a friend posted a card to me on December 1st and I received it on 16th January. Have had a lot of trouble with deliveries since I have lived here, some cards I have never received.

When I think as a child we had five deliveries a day all for one penny.

Talking of postage brings me to an instance concerning our postman, he parks his private car on our corner while he delivers our letters and lately our traffic wardens are being very strict and were about to have his car towed away. When he saw them he literally went on his knees and begged them to give him another chance, someone should have had a camera.

1993

Well, we have had one of the best winters for years, no snow, only a little fog now and again. My birthday this year was very quiet, no celebrations like last year. Had friends in for coffee and two neighbours brought in cards, had twenty-five and this year, they seemed exceptionally nice. Last year bought myself a birthday present, a lovely statuette of Jesus and two little children, called the Children's Blessing, it is so beautiful and stands on my television.

I heard this funny story the other day, told to me by my hairdresser and it is true. A lady came into his salon and asked for a shampoo and set, he asked her did she want a front or back wash? She thought for a moment then said, 'I would like it all washed.'

Going to a well known department store recently and buying some slippers, the carrier bag had printed on it, 'Your free carrier bag with our compliments' (how kind).

We have had several robberies here lately and we thought we were secure, a lovely mirror and four pictures and a plant from the lounge, musical items, they even whipped up two ladies' handbags while sitting in our lounge. One lady had her key in her bag which meant having a new lock and about 100 new keys, two days after the new lock was fitted someone put super glue in the lock. Crime and nothing but crime seems to be the order of the day, which brings me to the point how our courts sentence wrong-doers, 9 months for careless driving and killing four people and freed after only 4¹/₂ months, £40 fine for killing four people. £500 fine for dropping litter, it was always said the law was an ass, it might well be called a donkey.

I would scarcely think there is a household that hasn't had

either a robbery, mugging or some intrusion, it seems to me we have lost our freedom, freedom to go out at night, leave windows open and not have to keep a chain on the door or to take a handbag with you. Years ago I would leave work about 6 o'clock and would walk home through the downs even if it was foggy.

Changing Life Style

What a number of happenings change our life style, when we are young going to school, then to the big world of earning our living and learning about life, perhaps changing your job which means a different route to travel, getting married and into family life, moving to another district, losing one's partner, when perhaps you have been so used to getting in the car and being driven to where you want to go, and then cooking for only one. If you become handicapped in some way and not able to do the things you used to do, cannot walk much maybe and have to depend on some form of transport, in spite of what some folks say that they are independent, one cannot be wholly independent, we all need someone some time.

So many of my friends have moved these last few months, one of them our minister and his wife, he has retired, he was with us for ten years and very well liked and at his farewell the congregation showed their appreciation in the compliments they paid him and raised over £600 for a present.

My good friend Kathy has moved to a very nice flat officially opened by the Duke of Edinburgh and I have a lovely photo of them shaking hands.

Also Evelyn and Norman have moved to Sussex.

Some friends of mine have bought a house and were contemplating having a toilet made downstairs, there was one upstairs, but it is a wise decision to have one up and one down. Anyway they got in touch with a builder, a real old countryman he seemed to be. 'Well!' he said, 'it all depends on the pipe yer 'as, there's a wide pipe and a narrer pipe, corse if yer 'as the narrer pipe it's only fit for number one.' (No more need be said.)

Every incident recorded in this book is true and to read about the funny side of life, well if they give a moment's pleasure they are worth writing.

Now, I have always said I like living in a busy area, like looking out of the window and seeing folks and traffic, in other words like seeing a bit of life, especially as I am practically housebound. Well! I have certainly got my wish. I live nearly on the corner of a main road, traffic coming and going in four directions with a 30 and 56 bus service, there are four sets of obelisks which invariably get either knocked down or cars knock them sideways, we have several high lamp standards and one very careless driver knocked one right over a small enclosure where there are two seats, narrowly missing one of our residents who was sitting there, and breaking it in half. Several times we get police sirens. Sometimes in early morning we seem to get an endless stream of aircraft and often get a helicopter circling round for about 15 to 20 minutes looking for someone. Then sometimes there is complete silence, only for a few seconds and I listen to the quietness. Hardly a week passes that we don't get the fire brigade here, one only has to burn a piece of toast to set off that terrible alarm bell.

1994

On the 26th February we celebrated Margery's 80th birthday and it was a lovely occasion with all her relatives there, extra nice for us, Kathy, Olive and Rose because David kindly takes us and brings us home, they took a video of it and it was put on when we visited them later on.

Being dependent as I am on transport there are the odd occasions when they let you down and is very annoying, especially if you have an appointment which I had one day to go to the dentist. As Dial-a-Ride didn't turn up I rang for a taxi,

I have a card. They also didn't come after ringing them twice, so rang for a mini-cab, eventually all three turned up at the same time so chose Dial-a-Ride, that's what you call service.

Speaking of Dial-a-Ride it is very enjoyable when you go over ground you knew years ago and even see places you didn't know existed, in one part of our neighbourhood, the Richmond Road area, there are many roads named after trees and woods, Forrest, Mayfield, Beechwood, Mapledene, Greenwood, Laurel, Pine, Oak, Willow, Sycamore, Lavender, Ferncliff and Roseberry.

I do find it difficult when shopping as several items I need are on the top shelf so look round for someone tall to ask for help and it is always willingly given. Not so with a friend of mine who asked someone and got the reply, 'Get it yourself.' I cannot raise my arms up far or turn my neck round properly and have lost over an inch in height, but try to make the best of myself by wearing nice clothes and accessories that match.

I was talking to a neighbour the other day and she was telling me when her grandson came to visit her she was ashamed to be seen with him, his shoddy unkempt appearance, torn denim jeans and unshaved, she asked him if he needed any money to get a razor, Oh! no he replied.

Now we have another rail strike on Wednesday 15th June, whoever is at fault it is the long-suffering travelling public who bear the brunt.

We had our holiday to Eastbourne in June with Kathy and Olive, weather left a lot to be desired. Evelyn and Norman came on the Monday and took us to Alfriston then came back and had dinner with us which was very nice, but I was not well enough to enjoy it all.

The reason I felt unwell was, I had as I thought neuralgia, in fact all my teeth seemed to ache, earache and stabbing pains all over my head, one side of my face came out in red bumps and was very sore, also an open sore near my lip which was burning. I thought of shingles, and really felt ill and had lost my appetite, felt such a sight kept to my flat all week. I had made an appointment with my dentist but had to cancel it. My doctor gave me antibiotics and another doctor came and gave me some cream, still didn't known what it was and they didn't seem to know either. Feeling a little better I took two taxis to the dentist who was on holiday but saw his partner who took two X-rays and said there was nothing wrong with my teeth. Our holiday was approaching though I didn't feel like going. A friend said why not get another opinion, so did just that and took the opportunity while at Eastbourne.

The hotel manager was very kind in phoning for an appointment and said when I was ready he would ring for a taxi. Anyway on seeing the doctor he felt the back of my neck and said I had arthritis which I already knew and gave me some painkillers so that was a wasted effort.

At the hotel I got chatting with a mother and son who we see every year and he told me had had the same thing and how painful it was and was called the Trigeminal nerve. It is strange but it brings a degree of comfort to know someone else has had your trouble. After returning home I visited my dentist and he confirmed that was what it was, a virus related to chicken-pox and will take about six months to recover. At time of writing (August 1994) I have had it nearly four months. I feel quite well in myself but the right side of my face is still very sore and cannot even stand the sheet to touch it, have lost half a stone. To think I had seen three doctors and not one of them told me what it was.

'MY WEEKLY' 6/8/1994

My doctor gave me drug treatment for trigeminal neuralgia, but it hasn't worked. What else is there to try?

Trigeminal neuralgia causes severe, stabbing pain in the cheek, lips, gums or chin on one side of the face. The reason for it isn't certain and attacks can be triggered by washing, shaving, eating or drinking.

Drug treatment is usually helpful, but if not, go back to your doctor and he may suggest referral to a surgeon, as surgical techniques are available.

On the 20th August Kathy and I went to Worthing.

We had a very nice holiday, weather not too bad.

Visited the Connaugh Theatre and saw J.B. Priestly's 'Dangerous Corner', did several odd jobs of shopping and on Thursday Evelyn and Norman took us to what we thought was Roundstones, a very large garden centre, but we didn't quite make it and went to another one instead, they came back to dinner which finished off a very nice day.

We now have a new minister, Revd Lynda Hughes, and a deacon, Mr David Gallimore, both seem very nice and homely. Also a new Superintendent minister, Revd Gordon Squires, these changes always take place in September. After much controversy we have new chairs. Here, where I live we have had the roof repaired, one wouldn't have thought it was needed after only four years but the reason was bad workmanship in the first place, the whole place has been decorated, interior and exterior, not our flats, we are responsible for that. It's not surprising some firms go bankrupt when you see how work is carried out, my own flat door did not need doing but they painted it without undercoating it so it all had to be scraped off, then undercoated then painted, one door has been done five times, it seems the left hand doesn't know what the right hand is doing.

We have had a great deal of trouble with power cuts, sometimes caused by workmen severing a cable, how fortunate those folk who have gas, at least they can have tea and cook a meal, when you are all electric everything stops, to get up in the morning and find you cannot have your usual tea and toast is very disappointing. You cannot use the lift and it takes me nearly ten minutes to climb up 46 stairs one stair at a time. We have had many of these power failures, the electricity men repaired it and said they couldn't guarantee it would last, which it didn't and so it went on.

Now they say if you want anything done go to the top so I rang our director explaining everything and asked if there was anything he could do. He came down right away and got on to the electricity board, the men found the fault and since then we have been back to normal.

Our annual bazaar was a success, we advertise otherwise you don't get many people, I took over £65 and already had £30 in hand from odd jobs of work through the year. I also sell a few things here where I live and send that money to a charity. Now we have Christmas to look forward to which I love, writing the cards, about 70, doing up presents and various friends in for a chat all very enjoyable. Here is an amusing little story I heard on television, Jesus led his disciples down to the lakeside, a little boy said, 'Mummy! when we went to Lakeside we didn't see Jesus.'

I have come to the conclusion I must be an unusual person in my likes and dislikes for I find pleasure in many things other folk detest, like washing up, washing, ironing and unpicking, writing letters, doing Christmas cards, wrapping Christmas parcels and making order out of chaos. You don't come across many people who like moving but I don't mind at all. I do not agree with shopping on Sundays and Good Friday, surely time can be found on the other six days especially as some stores are open till 8 o'clock. Years and years ago my mother said if shops were open all night someone would shop, sure enough it showed on television a woman shopping at 3 a.m. in a super-market.

Hero Worship

It's a funny old world isn't it? I always thought to be classed as a hero you would have accomplished a brave deed, helped someone, saved someone, but must have got it all wrong, to be a hero you may well have been a gangster when you terrorised people and murdered someone, then when you die you get a right royal send-off as they say, thousands of people throng the street, numerous floral tributes and cheering all along the way. What an example to set our young people.

Pretty Woman

I was sitting next to an elderly lady in a waiting room the other day, she wanted to talk, strange how some folk want to unfold their life story to a complete stranger, she had lost her husband years ago and said she had had no children. She asked had I? I replied I was single, she turned to me astonished saying, 'What! a pretty woman like you, so elegant.' Now I have been told more than once about being elegant but pretty never, not with any stretch of the imagination could one say I was pretty, not even my best friends, but as the saying goes 'Beauty is in the eyes of the beholder'.

Giving and Receiving

I saw a heart-warming documentary story on the Esther Rantzen programme about a hospital in Russia that was literally falling to pieces. An army of volunteers from England gave eight days of their time to refurbish the hospital, painters, decorators, plasterers, electricians, plumbers, including some women. How hard they worked, new electrical equipment, baths and wash basins and toilets, gleaming walls with murals of cartoon characters in children's ward, and when a little boy pressed the lever to flush the toilet he was so scared to see the water rising he tried to stop it. When all was completed they had a celebration and gave toys to the children and the joy of the givers was as great as the receivers.

Blessings

Blessings, yes we all have them and you can count them, for

myself although I have arthritis like so many other people even babies. I have it in my neck, legs, arms and feet, cannot reach up or bend down or turn my neck round properly, my feet so the chiropodist tells me won't go where I want them to go and to rise from a chair is an effort. When I go to another person's house and they say sit down always look for the highest chair. I still manage to do my housework, except windows. Oh! how I wish I could kneel down to do my kitchen floor instead of using a mop. I am also troubled at times with high blood pressure, always associated B.P. with stress, not so in my case, I couldn't lead a more peaceful and easy life, unless it is stress of years ago catching up on me and yet my dreams show an anxious mind. Going back to blood pressure (prostrate hyper tension) the first time I experienced it, it really scared me, as soon as I lowered my head on the pillow everything whirled round and I clung to the bed which felt as if it was going round and round, I am thankful to say this only lasts a few moments, but is most frightening. Back to blessings, I can still do my embroidery and other bits of needlework although I have to stop now and again because of cramp and pins and needles in my hand, but to me the greatest blessing of all is I can 'see'.

I have just returned from a lovely Easter Sunday morning service taken by our deacon, who kindly took and brought me home as I was unable to get Dial-a-Ride. There was a wooden cross on a small table with wire around it and everyone took flowers up and threaded them through the wire, the results was beautiful and quite unique. Hope to get a snap of it.

6th, 7th and 8th May 1995
Celebration

What a wonderful weekend, the 50th Anniversary of V.E. day on the BBC, a joyous occasion to celebrate the peace of the Second World War.

Saturday: The Queen Mother joins 2,000 war veterans in Hyde Park, then the State Banquet at the Guildhall with visiting Royal Kings and Queens and Heads of State.

Sunday: A thanksgiving service at St Paul's Cathedral then a walk-about with the Queen and her family.

In the evening there was a Celebration Concert in Hyde Park with Vera Lynn and others.

Monday: The celebrations continue in Hyde Park with speeches of Winston Churchill read by Robert Hardy. A choir and massed bands with a medley of wartime songs with Dame Vera Lynn, Sir Harry Secombe and Cliff Richards. The Queen Mother then led her daughters on to the balcony to watch a fly-past of the Red Devils. There was a two minutes silence.

In the evening a Royal Gala and fireworks. The Mall and everywhere was thronged with people. A weekend to celebrate indeed, it was a tonic and also very moving as we shall never forget all those who gave their lives to save us.

The coverage of the BBC and all those who saw to the arranging of it all deserve to be congratulated also, and we were blessed with lovely weather.

Eastbourne Holiday 1995

The 3rd June Kathy and I went to Eastbourne but the weather wasn't kind to us, we only had one fine day the first week, luckily when Evelyn and Norman came and took us out to Alfriston, again we had tea in the 'Singing Kettle' very quaint as it is all around. We then went on to Beachy Head and Birling Gap and they came back with us and stayed to dinner. We went to the theatre and saw 'Suddenly at Home' by Francis Durbridge) and a three hour ride on the Dotto Train, we were glad to get under cover as it was so cold, a strong wind and drizzle, some folks in the hotel asked for hot-water bottles.

We did not expect to stay another week, the reason was my companion was feeling in need of a longer rest so on the spur of the moment I suggested another week. That necessitated a lot of thinking about, firstly, could the hotel accommodate us? Yes! Kathy just had to change her room. Could our driver oblige? Yes! I did not have sufficient tablets so wrote to my doctor for a prescription. My home-care was getting me some shopping on the Friday so rang her, my neighbour was taking in my milk, I was meeting a friend in Sainsbury's on Wednesday and the library was coming and Oh! my poor plants, but with phone calls and letters everything went smoothly, so handy to have phone numbers and addresses.

In spite of the weather and the grey days we enjoyed the break and the nice food all prepared and meeting old friends.

Worthing 12th–19th August 1995

The hottest summer on record, even hotter than 1976 and when it reaches the 90s it is a bit too much for most people, no rain for weeks which enforces water rationing in some parts. It was pleasing to have a lovely breeze on the coast, we saw more holiday makers than usual and a fair number of grandparents with their grandchildren, some staying at the hotel. We did some shopping, went to morning service at the church on our corner on the second Sunday had a coffee there, sat on the front and in Steyne Gardens opposite our hotel, where I sat with my parents eighty years ago.

Evelyn and Norman took us to Roundstones, a huge garden centre, we would have enjoyed it more if it hadn't been so hot, especially Kathy who was not feeling well, and they came back and had dinner with us.

Gerald Harper was staying at the hotel but we did not see him. It was a lovely holiday and we arrived home in record time, 2 hours from door to door, came over Hammersmith Bridge, through Richmond Park and didn't see any deer. Oh!

Harvest, 22 September 1996.

how lovely to be home and in time to see 'The Final Tribute' of V.J. day some fifty years ago, all very well organized as usual.

On the dais the Queen and Prince Philip, the Prince and Princess and their two sons, so close yet so far apart. The last big parade, the march past nearly a mile long in the heat of 88 degrees, elderly and old men and women, some sad, some with smiles on their faces, 'Veterans on Parade', the choirs and children with their long electric torches, a momentous occasion, and however one tries to forgive, when you see grown men weep thinking of their comrades who never returned, prisoners working on that terrible railway starved and beaten in the heat of 120 degrees it is very hard.

A few weeks before I went on holiday I had the pleasure of a visit from an American couple, a minister and his wife who were over here on an exchange visit while our minister stayed at their home in Washington. They were a delightful couple and I enjoyed the evening very much, exchanging our different way of life, they wanted to know all about both wars and the depression of the early thirties how we managed, they were so interested we could have talked for hours. When I explained what life was like here today, people not caring to go out after dark, locking doors and windows if you lived on the ground floor, they were surprised and said they could leave their door open. When I wheeled in the tea-trolley she said they would call that a cart.

No Beaches in London

I was chatting to a chambermaid while at Eastbourne about the lovely weather and she said she thought we would have a heat-wave. I said I didn't like too hot weather, but it would be cooler here than in London, she replied, 'Aren't there any beaches in London?'

Coming out of the church Sunday morning while on holiday I decided to sit in the gardens which are opposite. I was conscious of footsteps behind me and suddenly a gentleman said, 'I saw you in the church this morning.' I replied I was sure I had seen him, he went on to say he was in difficulties and wondered if any one could help him, he had received an urgent phone call and came out without any money. I said 'Why didn't you ask someone in the church?' He said it was locked up now which it was. I said would £5 help, he hesitated so I offered £10, he said he could return it. I then said I would have to pop in my hotel (which is also opposite) to get it as I don't carry much cash with me. He quickly said, 'Oh! no no am sorry I asked you,' and made a hasty retreat. Now was he genuine or not? I shall never know but have my doubts.

A Woman's Lot

The following chapters recall what life was like in the early nineteen hundreds and before, for the housewife, women's work was never done. The usual routine in winter would be to get the fire going, the focal point in any room. If it was an open fire or range you raked out the ashes and sifted the cinders to use again, blackleaded the grate and sometimes hearthstoned the hearth, laid the fire with newspaper and wood, either that you had chopped yourself or you could buy bundles of wood at the oilshop, small pieces of coal, strike a match to it and hope for the best. Sometimes it just wouldn't get going and you had to start all over again. If you had a range with an oven at the side you could do your baking, it would heat your water and burn a lot of your rubbish, and was lovely to toast muffins or crumpets using a long handled fork. There would be a coal scuttle at the side, sometimes in polished copper. The coal was delivered by a horse drawn cart, in $1/2$ or 1 hundredweight sacks, by dropping it down the chute, a round opening either in the forecourt or on the pavement covered by an iron grating, in a cupboard under the stairs or in a box on the landing. Wise people if of course they could afford it would have about three tons delivered in the summer when prices were cheaper. You also needed the sweep once or twice a year to sweep the chimney which necessitated the room being cleared and all remaining furniture covered over with dust sheets. If you neglected this the chimney could catch fire, and according to which way the wind was blowing you could get smoke coming into the room, some people had a cowl put on top of the chimney pot to stop it. Sometimes the sweep would ask you to go outside and see the brush coming out of the chimney to assure you he had done his job properly. Adjoining the kitchen if you lived downstairs would be a scullery with the sink, gas cooker and copper which you lit like a fire to boil your clothes in and at Christmas to boil the puddings.

Washing Day

Washing day was usually on a Monday and was not a happy day, especially if it was wet, when everything had to be dried indoors and the family not too pleased having washing hanging on lines across the room.

After boiling the whites and doing the remaining things some items needed starching, this needed very careful mixing else it would go lumpy (same as when you made a blancmange), damask tablecloths and tray cloths and lace curtains, also in the last rinsing of the whites you would use a blue bag, a little block of blue dye you squeezed into the water. On a fine day the washing would hang in the garden with the lines propped up, it would have a good blow and smell fresh. After washing you put things through the mangle to get most of the water out and when dry you mangled sheets and flat articles to make them smooth. There was only bar soap and soap flakes and maybe Hudsons Powder, used on a rubbing board. In a more affluent household bed linen would go to the laundry and men's stiff white collars to the collar dressers or you would have a washer woman in. A woman took pride in her washing.

Probably the evening would be spent doing any mending or darning socks ready for ironing which would be done by an iron heated on the fire or gas ring and put into a shield, it constantly had to be reheated, for anything with a frill a goffering iron was used, similar to what they used for Marcel hair waving. It was a day with a cold dinner of meat left over from the Sunday joint. If you lived upstairs you maybe had two flights of stairs to go up and down for every drop of water for washing, washing-up, cooking and bathing.

Baking Day

Many wives made their own bread, cakes, pies and puddings, it was not considered right to buy shop cakes. People went shopping more often as there were no refrigerators so food did not keep, if you had a larder or cellar they were cool. Most folk had a meat safe a wooden cabinet with shelves with perforated zinc door and sides. A baker would call every day and the milkman two or three times a day, early morning a zinc can with a handle, mid morning you took a jug for a pint or more and it was ladled from a churn. One thing you could be sure of seeing on the kitchen dresser was a set of three jugs. In the very hot weather you would boil the milk to save it turning sour or use earthenware milk coolers.

The Best Room

Sometimes called the best room, the front, the parlour and in some parts the Keeping Room, it was rather a sacred domain and only used Sundays or when guests arrived. It would have a carpet, a piano and a three piece suite covered in horsehair which was very prickly, bookshelves, maybe a whatnot in one corner and an overmantle over the fireplace, a brass fender and firearms, consisting of a long poker, brush and tongs which all had to be kept polished and when you did the carpet you would sprinkle wet tea leaves or small pieces of wet newspaper on to keep down the dust when you got down on your knees with a stiff hand brush.

The Bedroom

Lino on the floor with several rugs, a double bed, brass, including four knobs, it would have a mattress with a feather bed on top which had to be turned every day otherwise it would be lumpy and uncomfortable and maybe a Madras muslin curtain hung at the back. Most bedrooms were freezing cold in winter so you had a hot water bottle. A three piece suite consisting of a wardrobe, dressing table and a washstand with a jug and basin for washing, soap dish and tooth brush holder, and two china chamber pots in the compartment lower down and most likely a marble top.

After the oil lamp era, gas was installed for cooking and lighting, you used a very frail mantle on the gas jet and if you had a slot meter it often went out and you put another penny in.

A practical housewife would repair linen and clothing, not

because they were poor but it was the right thing to do not to be wasteful. After all there's no virtue in being extravagant, when sheets became a bit thin she would turn them sides to middles, turn collars on men's shirts and if she knitted her husband's socks would re-heel and toe them.

Most small houses had just one family but some people let the upper part, there were no bathrooms and only one toilet, often in the back garden which meant if there was no side door leading to the garden you had to pass through their kitchen even if it was mealtimes. Some householders kept a tin bath hooked on the garden wall and would bath in front of the fire, the water would be used for more than one person. In a more comfortably off home they would have a woman to do the washing, a charwoman as they were called to do the rough work, like outside steps which were kept scrubbed, and beat the rugs on the clothes-line with a carpet beater, a flat woven cane with a long handle. Such was life in those days, people accepted their lot because they didn't know any other way. You often hear people say, Young people don't know they're born. Quite true, I think compared with all the drudgery of the past when many tasks today are achieved by pressing a button.

Now in Victorian times if you wanted to make a jelly all you had to do was dissolve some isinglass in a saucepan and stew some raspberries in another, turn a kitchen chair upside down and fix a cloth tied to each leg, making a well in which to drain the raspberries putting a basin underneath, this took some time. When drained you mixed juice and isinglass together and poured into a copper mould. Not forgetting after the jelly cloth had to be washed and all copper pans cleaned thoroughly with lemon rind to prevent verdigris, a green deposit that forms on copper.

As told by Kathy Staff in a 'Songs of Praise' programme all about Sunday Schools: her teacher said to her, when you come next week bring your name written on a piece of paper and a frock, when she told her mother she asked what sort of frock? 'I don't know,' Kathy replied. Anyway during the week her mother met the Sunday School teacher so she asked her what sort of frock. 'Oh!' replied the teacher,' what I said was, 'bring your name written on paper and address.' A good little story well worth repeating.

The Scavenger Press have had a respite lately from probing into the private lives of royalty and other prominent people and making their lives a misery, the beef scare has been front page news, known as mad cow disease. It appears part of the spinal cord if not removed from the animal can cause mental illness and even death and beef burgers and other beef products have been banned from school dinners and restaurants and other catering establishments, foreign countries will not purchase it, very worrying for the farmers.

A terrible tragedy occurred in Dunblane, Scotland, on Wednesday 13th March 1996, a massacre of fifteen infants and a teacher and many wounded by a gunman with four revolvers who had an obsession with guns. I don't think there was a dry eye in the whole country, very upsetting for everyone, you couldn't help but cry every time it was on television.

On looking back (a comfortable pastime with some older folks) I have been doing handwork and machining for bazaars and various good causes for seventy years, I started when I was about fourteen so perhaps it is not surprizing that am getting a little tired, one reason is I cannot use my right hand long holding a needle or pen.

Now there is much talk of the millennium and I wonder if I shall still be here, I doubt it.

Our Queen will be seventy on the 21st April God Bless her.

I have just completed seventy years doing needlework, machining on my faithful treadle which I had when I was 21, for charitable causes. These have included teacosies, cushion covers, relining coats and shortening garments and aprons galore hand-embroidered tablecloths and various odd jobs for church bazaars, children's homes and Oxfam to send overseas. I started when I was fourteen and have not finished yet.

A Story of the Good Old Days (about 1919)

A husband with a wife and two young boys and his wife expecting another child, decided to go to Canada with the idea of finding work and getting a home together then he would send for his family, but no more was heard of him. His poor wife unable to work and penniless, contacted some comfortably off relatives to ask if they could help her by taking in one of the boys till after her confinement when she would then be able to work. They replied they were sorry they couldn't help her but they did send her a sack of potatoes.

After the baby was born, a little girl, the mother went out to work from six o'clock in the morning till 9 o'clock at night. When the daughter reached the age of twenty-one she tried to trace her father through the Salvation Army. They did trace him in Montreal, but they never heard any more of him. The daughter grew up to be a hard working church worker and looked after one brother till he died.

Living with Arthritis

This chapter is all about living with arthritis, so if it's likely to depress you don't read it. There are so many of us who suffer from it in one form or another, even little children. Mine is the crippling kind which bends your bones, so my back, legs and feet are curved, I am not a very elegant figure. When I awake on a day when I am not going out I feel a certain amount of relief although I love being out. When I approach a kerb I do not know which foot to put down and am grateful to take someone's arm if available. Using Dial-a-Ride is my only means of going out, to church Sunday, morning shopping once a fortnight, dentist and sometimes to see friends, the drivers are all very helpful.

When I write or sew I have to stop after a while because my fingers go numb. I would not trust myself to take my breakfast tray into my bedroom so use my tea-trolley. If I drop anything it needs a great effort to pick it up, it's surprising what a great help a kitchen fork is. To reach anything on a shelf is another problem and have to support my right elbow with my left hand, even to wash my neck or clean my teeth I use the same method. To put on a winter coat, what a struggle to get my other arm in.

To those of you who watch 'Brookside' on T.V. there was an episode in which a mother who had severe arthritis walks her daughter down the aisle on her wedding day using two sticks, suddenly her leg gives way and by some miracle she manages not to fall. I known exactly how that feels and often say a silent prayer when I need to walk from place to place.

It is strange, although it's such a trial to go on living day by day one still enjoys life and if you count your blessings you do have them if you think about it.

May 2000

After a few years I have taken up my pen again and now have great difficulty in writing as my hands go numb so after a few lines have to stop. I have just come upstairs from our lounge (am in a sheltered block of flats) where we had a young woman who gave a talk on how we ran a home years ago and I found it most interesting. It is strange, although people of my generation know it all, it is enjoyable to recall how we used to live. We were shown a heavy iron, a mincing machine, Sunlight soap and a blue bag to keep your clothes white, a goffering iron (like curling tongs we used to use) for ironing frills, the toasting fork and numerous other articles. Then the lady held up a document and asked had we seen one before, a bank statement hand written. There was a titter from the audience as hardly anyone ever had a bank statement, handwritten or otherwise. Looking back one wonders how we coped without the labour saving gadgets we have today.

Yesterday was a sad day, the funeral of a very dear friend Kathy, cousin of Margery, another good friend. They were and are the nicest people one could wish to meet and with Olive we had many enjoyable holidays, never any tension or unpleasantness, but all good things come to an end.

The funeral was at Manor Park, there were two cars and a private one with 17 followers, a lovely service at our church and back to where she lived where the warden put on a very nice spread for us. I could not speak my thoughts so wrote a message which Beaty read out at the service: 'Kathy was a true, helpful and loyal friend always reliable and I shall miss her very much and regret I could not visit her in hospital. Now after all her suffering she is at peace and I have the memories of the happy times we shared together, God be with you.' Also a tribute to Margery her beloved cousin who has been given strength to carry on during this trying time. She died on 15th October and would have been 79 on 25th November.

Our Postal Service

One wonders what has happened to our postal service these days, it has deteriorated beyond belief these last few years, sometimes only one post a day, anything from 12.30–2.00, sometimes 3 o'clock on a Saturday. Postmen who don't now how to put a letter in the letter-box without bending it in half, holiday cards are not quite the same with a crease down the middle, or Christmas and birthday cards. Wrong letters put in wrong doors. I am unfortunate in my address, that it has the same name as the road that runs alongside of it so I get mail for Navarino Road and they get mine for Navarino Mans. Gone are the good old days when we had four or five deliveries a day, what price progress. A friend of mine posted a letter 1st class to the next road and it took six days to get there, also in some districts pillar boxes are so full you could take out other letters.

I have had a worrying time recently, our Council have stopped my home-care visits, which I had twice a week for housework, laundry and shopping and getting my pension. I had a very nice person to do it, Agnes, because I don't need personal care such as help with bathing etc. I have been given a list of agencies to take your pick and pay a very high price I have made up a little story about it.

Oh! What a Rotten Job

Interviewing a young woman, I asked her what her occupation was, she replied she was a Social Service interviewer of the elderly regarding their needs. 'Do you enjoy your job?' I asked. 'Well, no not always. Today for instance I had to tell an 88 year old woman who can hardly walk and has not the proper use of either arm or hands that we would not be sending her a Home-Care worker any more.' 'Oh! What a rotten job,' I said.

I managed to get fixed up with an agency TLC (Tender Loving Care) and had a nice lady to do my work but the price is a bit steep. Anyway I wrote to my local paper about it and it aroused a lot of interest in such treatment, including an M.P. After numerous phone calls and letters, H. Council are going to send me someone.

Year 2000

After years of talks and planning about the Dome one wonders if the building of it was a worthwhile project. At the time of writing it doesn't seem very favourable, not to mention the cost. What I would have liked to have seen was a statue of Christ on the cliffs of Dover. Let us not forget that in spite of all the foreign tongues and cultures this is England, a Christian country, or was, a place where people flee to when ousted from their own land.

Also at the time of writing house property is so expensive it is beyond the reach of many young couples, everyone doesn't earn fabulous wages so some of them are going over to France because houses are cheaper. What a disgrace when we cannot provide for our own people. If you want a new car it pays to go abroad to get one.

One has to get on a soap box now and again.

On the evening of June 1st we saw the opening of our new church, I was taken by car and brought home by a minister and his wife. It all seems very nice but not an easy entrance, one has to park round the corner.

Have just seen a lovely service at St Paul's Cathedral to celebrate the Queen Mother's 100th birthday, although her birthday is not till August 4th.

I think everyone must have held their breath when she walked down those steps using one stick and holding onto the handrail they had fixed up for her. Also a Pageant on the 18th July which was lovely.

Now I am waiting for Vera to come in for tea and a chat, she has been very good to me over the years and often gets me odds and ends of shopping.

I have just had a visit from Christine, the librarian, to say they won't be calling regularly on Thursdays and may call any day or evening as their staff have been cut.

It is so nice to have books delivered to your door and occasionally one gets a book so absorbing that you don't want to leave it.

Now I really think I must bring this story to a close, an uneventful life one might say but a happy one in the main. Hoping all readers will enjoy it as much as I have in writing it.